TEACHER'S MANUAL

AMERICAN
PERSPECTIVES

READINGS ON CONTEMPORARY U.S. CULTURE

SUSAN EARLE-CARLIN
COLLEEN HILDEBRAND

Longman

Susan Earle-Carlin, University of California, Irvine (earlecar@uci.edu)
Colleen Hildebrand, University of California, Irvine (colleen@uci.edu)

American Perspectives: Readings on Contemporary U.S. Culture, Teacher's Manual

Pearson Education, 10 Bank Street, White Plains, NY 10606

Editorial director: Allen Ascher
Executive editor: Louisa Hellegers
Development editor: Carolyn Viola-John
Director of design and production: Rhea Banker
Associate director of electronic production: Aliza Greenblatt
Production manager: Ray Keating
Managing editor: Linda Moser
Production editor: Martin Yu
Electronic production editor: Rachel Baumann
Senior manufacturing manager: Patrice Fraccio
Manufacturing supervisor: Edith Pullman
Text design: Rachel Baumann
Cover design: Rachel Baumann

ISBN: 0-13-087532-5

3 4 5 6 7 8 9 10–DPC–05 04 03 02 01 00

CONTENTS

Introduction

This teacher's manual for *American Perspectives: Readings on Contemporary U.S. Culture* includes answers to exercises as well as recommendations for teaching and suggestions for expansion activities. The cultural points are also expanded upon to provide additional information.

Overview of the Text

Chapter Introduction and Focusing In

The photo and chapter opening paragraphs are followed by three activities.

Each chapter opens with a photo that illustrates the theme. The quote under the picture gives insight into the American psyche and stimulates discussion.

- ◆ *Have students point out the connection between the photo and the quotation.*
- ◆ *Ask them to discuss what they know about the people quoted.*

The opening paragraphs of each chapter introduction provide background on the topic and show how it relates to American values. The last paragraph acquaints students with the authors and the readings.

- ◆ *Read this section as a class and discuss it before assigning the first reading to help students get a feel for the chapter.*

A question refers students back to the opening photo.

- ◆ *Allow students to work in groups or with partners to answer the question and to share responses with the class.*

A short quiz or group activity gets students thinking about what they already know about the topic. These exercises vary in format: true/false, matching, or short-answer quizzes and discussions of stereotypes and proverbs. The answers and additional information can be found in the back of the book beginning on page 271. In Chapters 2, 4, 8, and 9, this activity, called **What Do You Think?**, attempts to dispel some of the stereotypes about Americans. While there is always some truth to these beliefs, the Background Information for Responses sections (in the answer key) provide facts that clarify the issues and help students understand the reasons why these generalizations are sometimes made.

- ◆ *Have students take the quizzes alone and compare answers, or quiz one another.*
- ◆ *Provide time for small groups to discuss the stereotypes and proverbs.*
- ◆ *Encourage competition between groups.*

Vocabulary knowledge is activated by matching quizzes (**Test Your Word Power**) or expansion activities on idioms and expressions (**Expand Your Vocabulary**).

- ◆ *Ask students to do these activities alone and, with a partner, to check answers in the back of the book beginning on page 271.*

Readings

There are three readings in each chapter; each is followed by five activities, **Understanding the Reading, Using the Vocabulary, Thinking Together, Writing about It,** and **Reacting to the Reading.**
Each reading is introduced by background information on the topic and the author.

- ◆ *Discuss the photo and the preview and prediction questions as a group to help the readers focus in on the content before reading and to keep a purpose in mind while they are reading on their own.*
- ◆ *Teach students the strategy of looking over the **Understanding the Reading** questions before they read the passage so they can mark the text and answer them more efficiently later.*
- ◆ *Preview the vocabulary as a class before reading, or encourage students to read the selections through once for the overall meaning before stopping to check definitions.*

Since the readings are authentic texts, difficult words are numbered, italicized, and glossed at the bottom of each page. The terms and symbols used in the definitions are adj = adjective; adv = adverb;

idiom; n = noun (including a phrase with a separate listing as a noun in the dictionary, such as *remote control*); np = noun phrase (a noun with modifiers, such as *cyberspace pop*, which does not have a separate entry in the dictionary); n pl = a noun most commonly used in plural form; proper n = proper noun (specific name of a person, place, or thing, such as *the Great Depression*); v = verb; vp = phrasal verb (a phrase that includes a verb and a preposition or adverb, such as *tune in*).

Understanding the Reading

These activities focus on different reading skills, from short-answer comprehension questions to more challenging critical thinking tasks. Because of this, we do not advise changing the order of the readings. The focus is on one or two skills per chapter (finding facts and details, identifying topics and main ideas, making judgments and inferences, paraphrasing, distinguishing fact from fiction, and summarizing) with a review in the beginning of the next. Students are also continuously encouraged to try different reading strategies, such as predicting, skimming, scanning, annotating the text, charting information, and outlining. In Chapter 10, two comprehension tests cover all skills previously learned.

Using the Vocabulary

Vocabulary exercises reexamine both thematic and glossed vocabulary through activities that include synonym and antonym distinctions, word form analysis, dictionary usage, word classifications, word games, vocabulary in context exercises, and analogies. Again, these activities appear in order of difficulty. Students are often referred back to the text to examine the vocabulary in context. Every reading also has a vocabulary cloze activity that is designed to review and reinforce word knowledge.

- ◆ *Use the 5–10 word review as a quick vocabulary quiz on each reading.*
- ◆ *Encourage students to use a marker to circle important words and phrases or to put a mark in the margin for words that they would like to discuss in class.*

Reading Graphs, Charts, Maps, and Tables

Each chapter contains one collaborative task that focuses on interpreting graphic material, such as maps, charts, schedules, tables, or graphs. This material always relates directly to one of the readings.

- ◆ *Allow class time for students to complete the short-answer exercises in small groups.*

Thinking Together

These tasks provide additional collaborative activities that encourage students to apply the information from the reading in a different way. In some cases, they are more appropriate for a conversation class or a multi-skills class and might be omitted from an academic class that concentrates only on reading or writing.

- ◆ *Try to set up the groups with as much diversity as possible since these activities often ask students to compare the way something is done in the United States to the way it is done in other countries. Arrange the groups to ensure that all students will feel comfortable participating.*
- ◆ *Establish a format for checking and sharing the information so that students take this activity seriously, instead of turning it into a chat session.*

Writing about It

The three writing topics following each reading can be assigned for homework or used as in-class shortwrites. These exercises, which require students to summarize, compare, or report, relate directly to the readings themselves and require an understanding of the reading in order to write an adequate response; for this reason, they can also be used as comprehension quizzes. There is often an opportunity for students to write in the voice of one of the people they have just read about.

- ◆ *Encourage students to use their imagination.*
- ◆ *Expand this activity by creating a role play in which the students act out their responses.*

Reacting to the Reading

Like **Writing about It**, these topics can be used as writing exercises. In addition, since they elicit personal reactions, they can also be used for small-group discussions or debates.

- ◆ *Try to set up a classroom community in which students feel comfortable voicing their opinions and commenting on the beliefs and values evident in the reading.*

Keeping Track of Your Reading Rate

This timed reading activity, which has been included so that students can measure their reading rate, should take no more than five minutes. Each reading is 400 words. The first reading should be used to establish a baseline rate (there is a chart in the Appendix on page 267). The timed readings offer a reading strategy (**Tip**) to help students improve speed and comprehension.

- ◆ *Tell students that they should measure their progress against their own baseline rate, not against their classmates' (however, a rate of 200 wpm with a comprehension rate of 7/10 is a good goal to set).*
- ◆ *Spend time explaining the tips first so that students can test them out as they read.*
- ◆ *Do not use these exercises as graded tests or they will lose the desired effect of encouraging students to try to read more quickly.*
- ◆ *Tell the students not to look ahead to pre-read this section or cheat by looking back at the readings to answer the questions since this will invalidate the results.*

Making Connections

There are three activities in this section of each chapter, **Responding to the Reading**, **Editing Your Work**, and **Writing an Essay**, followed by a list of books, movies, magazines, and websites (**Finding More Information**). These activities give students the opportunity to apply what they have learned by formulating responses to short questions and/or writing a longer essay on the topic. How much they are used will depend on the nature of the course.

Responding to the Reading encourages personal reactions, similar to journal topics. In contrast to the **Writing about It** exercises which concentrate on the material specific to each reading, these critical thinking questions force students to think about the broader topic of the chapter and to consider how the readings help support a view of American culture. Students are also asked to examine the ideas they have read about in relation to their own experiences and cultures or to reexamine the quotes, facts, and statistics from the shaded boxes in the text.

- ◆ *Ask students in a writing class to keep a journal of these writing topics as a semester project.*

Editing Your Work provides writing instructors with a quick means to review a grammar point. The grammar points stem from the language in the readings and the language that will be elicited in the writing assignments. The paragraphs were written by students in response to the assignments in *American Perspectives* and are directly related to the theme of the chapter.

- ◆ *Use these exercises as collaborative editing activities, for homework, or for quick grammar quizzes.*
- ◆ *Remind students to edit their writing as they work on their essays.*

Writing an Essay expands the writing exercises into an essay. This section can be omitted in a class dedicated only to reading. The essay topics cover a wide range of rhetorical styles, from personal narratives and descriptions to research essays.

- ◆ *Encourage students to brainstorm in groups before they choose a topic so that they can discover which essay interests them most. For the first assignment, go over the brainstorming techniques on pages 262–263.*
- ◆ *Remind students to reexamine their shortwrites and journal writings for ideas.*
- ◆ *Show students how to integrate quotations and facts from shaded boxes smoothly into their essays.*

Finding More Information takes the readers beyond this text by providing titles of books, movies, and magazines as well as Web addresses. Information on many of the books and films listed can be found on booksellers' websites (http://amazon.com; http://borders.com). Reviews and information on movies can also be found at the Internet Movie Database http://us.imdb.com. The Web addresses provided in this section include as many permanent sites as possible (i.e., those from the government or established organizations).

♦ *Take your class to a computer lab to try out the websites and search for more information.*
♦ *If a URL doesn't work, try searching for the title of the page listed with the address.*

A Note on the Quotations and Facts in the Margins

The quotations in the margins all represent the voices of American writers, singers, politicians, and celebrities and help reinforce the students' understanding of American values and culture. The facts and statistics help support the ideas in the readings.

♦ *Tell students to look over the quotations, facts, and statistics in the shaded boxes to help them predict the overall theme.*

Scope and Sequence

The chart below summarizes the reading, vocabulary, and editing skills highlighted in each chapter.

Chapter	Reading Skills	Vocabulary Skills	Editing Skills
1	• recalling facts and details • reading maps	• descriptive phrases • synonyms	• verb tense
2	• recalling facts and details • charting information • reading tables	• synonyms/antonyms • vocabulary in context	• subject–verb agreement
3	• finding information • identifying topics • reading tables	• compound words • suffixes • word forms	• S endings
4	• understanding terms • listing and annotating • reading graphs	• dictionary skills • prefixes and roots • classifying words	• parallelism
5	• listing and mapping • understanding main ideas • reading maps	• vocabulary in context • participial adjectives • compound words	• participial adjectives
6	• stating main ideas • distinguishing fact/opinion • reading ads	• technical vocabulary • abbreviations and acronyms • phrasal verbs	• articles
7	• outlining • drawing conclusions • reading timelines	• suffixes and prefixes • analogies	• passive voice
8	• evaluating evidence • charting and summarizing • distinguishing myth/reality • reading schedules	• word forms • figurative language	• word forms
9	• paraphrasing • making inferences • sequencing • reading graphs	• hyphenated modifiers • classifying words • vocabulary in context	• verb forms
10	• reviewing skills • paraphrasing and summarizing • reading graphs	• figurative language • analogies	• verb tense

Answers to Preview Activity (page x)

1. ten **2.** Chapter 5 **3.** in footnotes **4.** four **5.** map of NY subway system (page 8) **6.** page xii, Text Credits **7.** possible answers from text credits page: "Return to Ellis Island" (page 4); "Is That Your REAL Brother?" (page 45); "The Special Olympics" (page 71); "Shape Up America! (page 93); "Jacques d'Amboise" (page 128); "Online Dating: Myth vs. Reality" (page 141); "The History of the American Red Cross" (page 162); "Jackie Robinson" (page 169); "Jackie Robinson" and "Online Dating: Myth vs. Reality" show the website on the page of the reading. **8.** possible answers: ahf.org; www.healthfinder.com; www.hhs.gov; www.phys.com (page 103) **9.** Appendix A: Suggestions for Reading and Writing; Appendix B: Idioms and Expressions; Appendix C: Keeping Track of Your Reading Rate; Appendix D: Map of the United States/State Mottoes and Postal Abbreviations **10.** See pages 261–264.

CHAPTER 1

Going Back to Our Roots

FOCUSING IN (pages 2 and 3, answers on page 271)

The photo is of an immigrant family looking at the Statue of Liberty, located in New York Harbor on Liberty Island. It was designed by the French sculptor Frédéric Auguste Bartholdi and dedicated in 1886. It was declared a National Monument in 1924. It is a global symbol of freedom and marks the arrival of immigrants to the United States. For the statue's centennial celebration in 1986, the large iron and copper statue was rehabilitated. The quote is from the poem "The New Colossus" by the American poet Emma Lazarus (1849–87), which was written specifically for the inscription on the Statue of Liberty. The complete text reads: "Keep, ancient lands, your storied pomp!" cries she / With silent lips. "Give me your tired, your poor, / Your huddled masses yearning to breathe free, / The wretched refuse of your teeming shore. / Send these, the homeless, tempest-tossed, to me; / I lift my lamp beside the golden door."

Can You Pass This "Citizenship" Test? (page 3)

Expansion: See if students know what immigrants need in order to become citizens of different countries. In the United States, they need to: be eighteen or older; be a permanent U.S. resident living continuously in the U.S. for five years and in one state for at least three months; have no record of breaking certain laws; show support for the principles of the Constitution of the United States; read, write, speak, and understand English; demonstrate knowledge and understanding of the history and government of the U.S.; and take the oath of allegiance, swearing to "support the Constitution and obey the laws of the U.S.; renounce any foreign allegiance and/or foreign title; and bear arms for the Armed Forces of the U.S. or perform services for the government of the U.S. when required." Sample questions on the multiple-choice citizenship test include "When did Christopher Columbus voyage to America?" "What were the first thirteen states called?" Sample citizenship tests can be found on the Internet at: http://www.rusam.com/immig/citiz/citiz_s.htm. If the class is taught in the U.S., have students interview a recently naturalized citizen to find out more about the process.

Expansion: According to the *LA Times*, 6/14/99, "Citizenship denials nationwide grew 251 percent during the first six months of the 1998–1999 fiscal year, compared to the same period a year earlier, U.S. Immigration and Naturalization Service records show." Have students discuss reasons why this might have been the case. [According to the article, reasons include lost files, computer problems with records, applicants' failure to respond, missing or incorrect addresses (which may result in missed interviews), inability to speak English, criminal records, and failure to pass the civics test.]

Return to Ellis Island Evokes Memories and Pride
Chuck Sambar, http://www.sambarpress.com (page 4)

Preview notes: Ellis Island is in New York Harbor. According to Sambar (par. 4), "For six decades, from 1892 to 1954, Ellis Island was the entry point to some 12 million people, 40 percent of our nation's population at the time."

Understanding the Reading: Recalling Facts and Details (page 7)

This exercise tests students' memory and comprehension of the details in the reading.

◆ *Point out that scanning is like looking in a phone book for a person's name and phone number; here students should pick out a key word or number to scan for when checking answers.*

Answers: **1.** 1952 (par. 1) **2.** Lebanon (par. 2) **3.** the Statue of Liberty (par. 1) **4.** 12 million (par. 4) **5.** more than 5,000 (par. 8) **6.** no (par. 8) **7.** ferry (par. 6) **8.** donation in his name to the restoration of Ellis Island (pars. 2, 11) **9.** immigrants who passed through Ellis Island (par. 12) **10.** *Island of Hope and Island of Tears* (par. 9)

Using the Vocabulary: Descriptive Adjectives (page 7)

An author's choice of adjectives helps him or her set the tone for a piece of writing.

♦ *Ask students to look over the list of words in the first column to see how the adjectives help readers better understand the writer's point of view.*

Answers: **1.** fortunate (b; par. 3) **2.** overwhelmed visually and emotionally (f; par. 9) **3.** anxious and tense (a; par. 6) **4.** lost, disoriented, uninformed (c; par. 9) **5.** innovative, interactive (g; par. 10) **6.** meaningful and sensitive (d; par. 12) **7.** grateful and proud (e; par. 13)

Reading Maps (page 8)

Working with graphic materials, such as this map exercise and the one on page 121 in Chapter 5, helps students pay attention to details and learn directional skills. The graphic materials in this text provide an opportunity for the visual learners to lead a group problem-solving activity.

Answers: **1.** the C and E trains **2.** South Ferry **3.** Brooklyn Bridge **4.** the 2, 3, 4, 5 trains **5.** Canal Street

Expansion: Have students bring in local maps or bus routes or maps of cities in their home countries. Ask them to make up five questions about the maps to use in a class map contest.

Thinking Together (page 9)

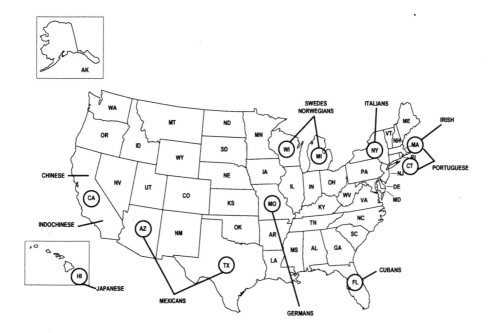

Reacting to the Reading (page 9)

National monuments in the United States are: The Lincoln Memorial and the Washington Monument in Washington, D.C.; The Statue of Liberty; Mount Rushmore in South Dakota. Monuments in other countries include: The Arc de Triomphe in Paris; the pyramids of Egypt and Teotihuacan in Mexico; the Great Wall of China.

For My Indian Daughter
Lewis P. Sawaquat, *Newsweek*, 9/5/83 (page 10)

Preview notes/suggestions: Native Americans were the first inhabitants of the American continent. As U.S. pioneers moved westward in the early 1800s, battles with the Native Americans were frequent and tragic. The U.S. cavalry helped defend settlers and in doing so decimated the Native American population. By the end of the nineteenth century, most Native Americans were forced onto reservations in states such as Utah, New Mexico, Arizona, and Colorado. Today reservations are governed by tribal law, not state laws, and Native Americans living on reservations are trying to reestablish their culture.

Understanding the Reading: Recalling Facts and Details (page 13)

Answers: 1. b **2.** b **3.** a **4.** c **5.** a **6.** b **7.** c **8.** b

Expansion: Ask students to explain how ethnic minorities, especially indigenous populations, are treated in other countries around the world.

Using the Vocabulary: Synonyms (page 14)

A. Answers: 1. *affluent* (rich) **2.** *culminated* (ended) **3.** *outfit* (military company) **4.** *bully* (overpower by force) **5.** *powwow* (meeting) **6.** *iridescent* (shining) **7.** *masquerade* (wear costumes and masks) **8.** *squinting* (peering out of half-closed eyes) **9.** *moronic* (foolish) **10.** *discomfiting* (upsetting)

B. Answers: 1. discomfited **2.** culminated **3.** powwows **4.** moronic

Thinking Together (page 15)

Cultural traditions that might be discussed here include holiday celebrations (Christmas, Tet, the Moon Festival, Cinco de Mayo), tea ceremonies, family reunions, naming ceremonies, baptisms, feasts to honor the dead, and traditional dress.

My Father's Black Pride
Marcus Bleecker, *The New York Times Magazine*, 10/15/95 (page 16)

Preview notes: Help students get started by bringing up the topics of language barriers, discrimination, acculturation, and religious differences.

Understanding the Reading: Identifying Facts and Details (page 18)

♦ *Remind students that* who *refers to a person,* what *refers to a thing,* where *refers to a place,* when *refers to a time, and* why *refers to a reason or explanation.*

A. Answers: 1. *Who*—his father **2.** *What*—African, Caucasian, Jewish **3.** *Where*—Princeton, NJ **4.** *When*—in college **5.** *Why*—because he wanted a role model for him

B. Answers: 1. Bleecker's father knew his children would face racism. (par. 3, sent. 4) **2.** Today, Bleecker has positive self-esteem. (par. 1, sents. 7–9) **3.** Bleecker is a jazz musician. (par. 5, sent. 4) **4.** Books were an important means of learning about heritage in the Bleecker family. (par. 4, sent. 1) **5.** Bleecker spent part of his childhood living among blacks. (par. 7, sent. 1)

Using the Vocabulary: Synonyms (page 19)

A. Answers: 1. shades (sunglasses) **2.** deny/disavow (ignore) **3.** genre (type) **4.** confrontations (fights) **5.** scowl (frown)

B. Answers: 1. deny/disavow **2.** epitomized **3.** confrontations **4.** predominantly **5.** bigotry

Thinking Together (page 20)

- ◆ *Have the class develop a list of appropriate questions to ask one another about their ethnic backgrounds.*
- ◆ *Encourage students to interact with students they do not usually talk to.*

Keeping Track of Your Reading Rate (page 21)

This reading serves to establish a baseline reading rate.

- ◆ *Since this is the first timed reading, explain to the students the benefits of improving their speed.*
- ◆ *Use a clock with a second hand for this activity.*
- ◆ *Go over the chart on page 267 that provides words per minute for each 10-second interval.*
- ◆ *Explain that you will mark down the time on the board at 10-second intervals and that they must look up and record the last time indicated as soon as they are done reading.*
- ◆ *Encourage students to follow the instructions and not to look back at the reading in order to answer the questions.*
- ◆ *After explaining the format, read the short introductory paragraph together and go over the hint before starting the timing.*

Answers: **1.** F (It took place on a university campus, UC Irvine.) **2.** T **3.** T **4.** F (Events took place throughout the day.) **5.** T **6.** F (Performances included Native American, Hawaiian, Scottish, Filipino, and Japanese songs and dances.) **7.** F (There was a variety of food from different cultures.) **8.** T **9.** T **10.** F (The rainbow symbolizes the diversity of colors and cultures.)

Making Connections—Editing Your Work (Verb Tense) (page 23)

- ◆ *Review verb tenses since students might be writing an essay about past experiences.*

    This is about an Indian family. The parents decided to come to America with the intention of getting jobs and giving their children a better education. Before they came to America, they had sold most of their property in their country. They thought they ~~can~~ **COULD** earn three or four times more money than what they were earning in India. When they first arrived in America, they ~~don't~~ **DIDN'T** know anybody in the country. The family stayed in a hotel until they ~~find~~ **FOUND** a place to live. As soon as they ~~move~~ **MOVED** to an apartment, they started to apply for jobs that were related to their fields, but they didn't succeed. At first, they were unsuccessful because they ~~don't~~ **DIDN'T** speak English well and their degrees in engineering were not valid in the state they were living in. Their pride and self dignity were hurt and too many doors were closed to their success.

CHAPTER 2
Changing the American Family

FOCUSING IN (pages 26 and 27, answers on page 271)

The photo on page 26 shows an American family gathering. It highlights the fact that Americans do celebrate holidays together in order to maintain family ties. The quotation is from Gloria Steinem, the founding editor of *MS* magazine and a strong feminist voice from the 1960s through the present. The quotation helps to show how diverse families are and how outsiders cannot easily understand the dynamics of family relationships. In fact, even family members themselves don't necessarily understand one another.

In this chapter, the first set of stereotypes include common perceptions that American families are falling apart, American children are disrespectful and rebellious, and the elderly are neglected.

Most of the information in the answer key comes from the U.S. Census Bureau (www.census.gov); a census is taken every 10 years.

What Is a Family?
Bernard Gavzer, *Parade*, 11/22/92 (page 28)

Preview notes: Bernard Gavzer is a syndicated columnist based in New York. His articles are often informative views of contemporary American society.

◆ *Allow students to share their answers to the title question. Explain that the meaning of "family" is a sensitive issue and can often be controversial because points of view differ among individuals within a country, as well as among individuals from different cultures.*

Understanding the Reading: Recalling Facts and Charting Information (page 32)

◆ *Emphasize that visual aids, such as the chart in Exercise B, can help organize information for later use.*
◆ *Provide the paragraph numbers in which students can find the information if they have trouble with the answers.*

A. Answers: 1. a. (par. 3) **2.** b. (par. 5) **3.** b. (par. 7) **4.** b. (par. 10) **5.** a. (par. 15) **6.** c. (par. 20) **7.** a. (par. 22) **8.** b. (par. 13) **9.** c. (par. 24) **10.** b. (pars. 26–27)

B. Answers: While the Cones typified "a marriage in the most traditional sense" in the 1950s, putting family before work is no longer always possible. Even though other answers for this exercise may be inferred, the family groups listed on the chart represent the most typical examples of each category as is seen in the article.

Being Accepted by Others	Being Unmarried	Being a Single Parent	Juggling Work and Family
Belser and White	Conway and Brunkow	Walker	Lawerence and Martin

Using the Vocabulary: Antonyms (page 33)

A. Answers: 1. adamantly - weakly **2.** attuned to - disconnected from **3.** batter - caress **4.** demise - growth **5.** gifted - average **6.** immune to - affected by **7.** resent - appreciate **8.** sensitive - unfeeling **9.** wane - increase

B. Answers: 1. juggle **2.** attuned **3.** resent **4.** flex time **5.** alimony

Reading Tables (page 34)

This exercise requires careful reading of the terms in order to give correct answers (mean = average; median = point at which half are below and half are above). For example, although the table here shows that the percentage of children being raised in single-parent families has increased, it does not show the actual number; and although the number of married adults in the United States increased between 1970 and 1997, we don't know if that represents a larger percentage of the population.

Answers: 1. F **2.** T **3.** F **4.** T **5.** T

Thinking Together (page 35)

Children should be seen and not heard and *Silence is golden* are proverbs that parents sometimes use to keep their children quiet. The former is used especially when adults are talking and they do not want to be interrupted. *Spare the rod and spoil the child* means that parents who do not punish their children will end up with children who are bratty and undisciplined. Other proverbs are *The apple doesn't fall far from the tree* (Children inherit the habits of their parents) and *An idle mind is the devil's workshop* (People who are kept busy stay out of trouble).

Expansion: Make a list of proverbs (including those from this chapter) numbering half of your class size. Write one half of each proverb on a slip of paper. Put the papers in a box at the front of the class. Have each student pick one slip. Give them time to walk around the class to find the student with the matching half of the proverbs. Ask them to explain the meanings of the proverbs to the class.

It Takes a Strong Person to Survive Life on the Daddy Track
Dennis McLellan, the *Los Angeles Times*, 8/20/95 (page 36)

Preview notes: According to an *LA Times* (1999) survey, 69 percent of the 2,021 California residents polled (both men and women) agreed that "It is much better for a family if the father works outside of the home and the mother takes care of the children."

◆ *Ask students if they agree with the people surveyed. Point out that this issue is widely debated in the United States.*

Understanding the Reading: Recalling Facts and Discussing Details (page 39)

Answers:
1. They want their children raised by one of the parents (Harris, par. 17); the wife has a better job and benefits (Boylan, pars. 23–24); more flexible job and time (Ross, par. 4; Garrett, par. 27)
2. They feel alienated (pars. 10–11); they want the support of others in the same situation (par. 21).
3. Women get angry (par. 2); people make fun of them (par. 3); people think they are strange or that there is something wrong with them (pars. 6, 7, 12, 13, 20).
4. The fathers talk via America Online at 7 P.M. Pacific Daylight Time (PDT) on Mondays (par. 22).
5. Dicenzo, social service worker (par. 7); Harris, cook, photographer, catalog designer (par. 16); Baylies, software engineer (par. 19). Note: Ross, a musician/composer, and Boylan, an actor, didn't necessarily give up their jobs to be full-time dads.

Using the Vocabulary: Synonyms and Antonyms (page 39)

A. Answers:

Column A	Column B	S (Synonym) / A (Antonym)
suspicion	trust	A
nagging	annoying	S
respect	admiration	S
acknowledge	ignore	A
inevitable	unavoidable	S
unemployed	working	A
ego	self	S

B. Answers: 1. nagging **2.** acknowledges **3.** respect **4.** suspicion **5.** inevitable **6.** unemployed
C. Answers: 1. sufficient **2.** wives **3.** relate **4.** useful **5.** willingly

Thinking Together (page 40)

◆ *First, as a class, list household duties/chores that need to be done to run a home. Have students use this list to fill in the chart by determining whether the chores are done by fathers or mothers in their countries.*

Expansion: Have students interview their grandparents to see how gender roles in families have changed.

Writing about It (page 40)

◆ *Remind students to review their answers to **Understanding the Reading** when writing their paragraphs.*

Reunions Keep Families in Touch with Roots

Marcia Schnedler, the *Salt Lake Tribune*, 3/10/96 (page 41)

Preview notes: Explain the concept of a reunion to students. Since it is not uncommon for members of families to be spread out across the fifty states, planned reunions every five or ten years help keep families in touch.

Understanding the Reading: Scanning for Facts (page 43)

◆ *Remind students that scanning is looking quickly for something specific; in this case, all of the facts involve scanning for a number.*

Answers: 1. *Roots* (par. 5) **2.** Bullock (par. 7) **3.** George Bullock Sr. (par. 8) **4.** Travel Industry Association of America (par. 3) **5.** Barbados (par. 9) **6.** 7 million (par. 4) **7.** the Gaither-Janes family reunion (par. 10)

Using the Vocabulary: Vocabulary in Context (page 44)

Exercises in Chapter 5 (page 111) will reinforce the development of this skill.

◆ *Explain to students that often the first step in figuring out a word from context is determining the grammatical function of the word in the sentence.*

◆ *Remind them to look for word endings, determiners, and modifiers as clues to parts of speech.*

A. Answers: 1. caterer—noun (par. 2) **2.** impromptu—adjective (par. 8) **3.** reconstituted—verb (par. 17) **4.** deceased—adjective (par. 16) **5.** intermarried—verb (par. 9) **6.** phenomenon—noun (par. 4)

B. Answers:

Word	Part of Speech	Definition	Sentence
get-together (par. 2)	noun	reunion, gathering of people	
scatter (par. 4)	verb	to move around	
evolve (par. 8)	verb	to grow or come about; develop	
excursion (par. 12)	noun	trip; visit	
seminar (par. 14)	noun	class	

C. Answers: 1. scattered **2.** get-togethers **3.** evolved **4.** excursions **5.** seminars

Expansion: Because figuring out vocabulary from context is such an important reading skill, you might want to duplicate this activity with words from this or other readings.

Thinking Together (page 45)

◆ *Have students vote on which family reunion sounds like it would be the most fun and rewarding and which one would be the most practical or feasible.*

Expansion: To encourage class participation and cultural awareness, plan a class event or trip.

Keeping Track of Your Reading Rate (page 45)

◆ *Go over the introductory information before starting the exercise, and review the tip which reminds students to activate their previous knowledge in order to anticipate what the author will say next.*

Answers: 1. T **2.** F (He was born in Michigan; Kerry jokingly says he comes from Mars.) **3.** F (The writer says "not being the particularly shy and reclusive type.") **4.** F (She didn't even realize she came from another country until she was in her teens and then she denied her heritage.) **5.** T **6.** F (Her parents often got together with other parents who had adopted Korean children.) **7.** T **8.** F (She speaks about her teen years in the past.) **9.** T **10.** T

Making Connections—Editing Your Work (Subject Verb Agreement) (page 47)

This exercise reviews the **S** ending on verbs with third-person singular subjects since students may be using the present tense to describe their families. The one-**S** rule is a good rule of thumb: With regular nouns and regular verbs in the present tense, there must be one and only one **S** ending, either on the subject or on the verb.

In *Parade*, the article by Gavzer **states** that traditional American families often **includes** "two parents, a father who works, and a mother who **raises** her two or three children at home." This is also true for traditional Japanese families. Japanese men want their wives to stay at home and take care of their children while they are out working very hard to support their families. Therefore it can be said that families in America and Japan **bases** their belief of a traditional family on the same points. But I also found some differences. Americans seem to date more people before marriage than Japanese people **does**. Although an American **experiences** many dates, this **doES** not make it any easier to marry the right person. Everybody have **HAS** a hard time picking the right person to be their husband or wife. In Japan there is **ARE** many networks that can arrange marriages for men and women. When the right person is found, the marriage **follows**.

CHAPTER 3

Leveling the Playing Field

FOCUSING IN (Pages 50 and 51, answers on page 272)

The photo on page 50 was donated by Colours by Permobil, a company that manufactures specially designed wheelchairs. With the advent of such wheelchairs, the possibility for athletes with disabilities to compete in sports events has grown. The first wheelchair athlete competed in the Boston Marathon in 1975.

The quote by Lewis H. Lapham (U.S. essayist and author of *Money and Class in America* and editor of *Harper's* magazine) captures many American values: youth, hope, optimism, and the triumph of good over evil.

Ready, Set, Go: Why We Love Our Games
Mike Tharp, *U.S. News and World Report*, 7/15/96 (page 52)

Preview notes: Although physical education (P.E.) classes are part of the curriculum throughout U.S. public schools, they vary from state to state. Often children have two or three hours of P.E. per week in elementary school (running; playing handball, tetherball, and basketball; swinging on bars), one hour daily through grades 7 and 8 in middle school or junior high, and one hour daily for the first two years in high school (running; playing basketball, volleyball, football, soccer, softball). However, according to Dr. C. Everett Koop, children do not get enough physical activity (see Chapter 4, page 94). As a result, 21 percent of American children (ages 12–19) are considered significantly overweight. Most high schools in the United States have competitive intermural teams, usually in soccer, baseball, football, and basketball. Parents raise money for teams and are active participants as coaches in soccer (A.Y.S.O.) and baseball (Little League).

Understanding the Reading: Identifying Information (page 55)

Y/N	Information	Phrase/Fact in Text and Paragraph Number
N	1. The number of people surveyed in the *U.S. News* poll.	only percents were given
Y	2. Most Americans in the *U.S. News* poll believed the government should support Olympic athletes financially.	par. 2; 2/3 think the Olympians should get government aid
Y	3. The name of the law that opened up sports for women in college.	par. 7; Title IX of the Education Amendments in 1972
Y	4. The author concludes that Americans believe sports figures are heroes.	par. 12; sports heroes represent "the best of who we are"
N	5. Most Americans polled had bad experiences with sports as children.	par. 11; only 1 in 10 did
Y	6. More than one-third of the athletes at the 1996 Olympics in Atlanta were women.	par. 5; almost 4,000 out of nearly 11,000
Y	7. Sports influence language and fashion.	par.3; "three strikes" laws and baseball caps
N	8. Americans in the 1996 poll believed girls and boys had the same opportunities to participate in sports.	par. 7; 75 percent said that girls do not have the same opportunity
N	9. The majority of Americans interviewed participated in sports at least twice a week.	par. 10; only 1/4 to 1/3 say they do
Y	10. Most people in the survey believed sports had a good influence on American life.	par. 4, 11, and 12; sports "contribute postively to other life realms" and "athletic participation helps a person succeed in business"

Using the Vocabulary: Compound Words (page 56)

A. These are only some of the many compound words found in this reading. Here all of the examples are one-word compounds. In Chapter 5, page 126, there is a review of compound words.

Compound Words	Definitions	Compound Words	Definitions
lifestyle (par. 1)	(n) way of living	scoreboard (par. 3)	(n) board on which points won in a game are recorded
worldwide (par. 1)	(adj/adv) universal; everywhere in the world	pocketbook (par. 3)	(n) a handbag or purse to carry papers and money
network (par. 2)	(n) group of radio or TV stations	otherwise (par. 3)	(adv) if not
baseball (par. 3)	(n) sport played by two teams; win points by hitting a ball with a bat	chairman (par. 3)	(n) a person in charge of a meeting or committee
football (par. 3)	(n) sport played by two teams; win points by throwing or kicking a ball through an opponent's goal	outside (par. 10)	(prep) not inside a room or building
basketball (par. 3)	(n) sport played by two teams; win points by throwing a ball through a net		

B. Answers: 1. lifestyle **2.** baseball **3.** football **4.** basketball **5.** network

Expansion: Ask students to scan paragraph 3 for more examples (*slam-dunks; audiovisual; all-sports; sports-specific; Internet-linked*).

Thinking Together (page 57)

◆ *List several popular sports on the board. Poll the class by asking questions like: "In which countries is soccer the most popular (number one) sport?" "Who has baseball listed as the second most popular sport?"*

◆ *Tally up the results for first, second, and third most popular sports. Discuss the results and have students share reasons why one sport is more popular than others.*

Baseball's All-Star Game: A Game by Game Guide
Jeff Lenburg, 1986 (page 58)

Preview notes: Find a student volunteer who can explain baseball to the class. Drawing a diamond on the board and explaining where the bases are might help. As the article explains, the All-Star Game is a yearly event that takes place in different ball parks across North America in July (a chart of scores and locations is on page 63). The two leagues (American and National) are not determined by geography or status. Cities have to have enough money to support a major league team and provide a stadium for it to play in. Some large cities have both American League and National League teams (New York—the Yankees and the Mets; Chicago—the White Sox and the Cubs). Others have only a National League team (the Los Angeles Dodgers); many have no major league teams at all.

The "democratic" features of the All-Star Game are these: There are a National League team and an American League team with players chosen by the fans; the managers of each team are the managers whose teams won their leagues and met in the World Series the previous October; the games alternate between National League and American League ball parks each year and follow the rules of that park.

Understanding the Reading: Identifying Topics (page 61)

Topics are phrases, rather than complete sentences, that state the overall theme or subject of a piece of writing. For example, the topic of this reading is the development of the All-Star Game. It would be too broad to say the topic is "sports" or even "baseball." It would be too narrow to say it is "the failure of Lane's idea" or "voting for the All-Stars." In this exercise, students are asked only to recognize topics; in the next reading, on page 65, they will write the appropriate topics for each paragraph.

B. Answers:

par. 1—f	par. 5—b	par. 9—g
par. 2—j	par. 6—h	par. 10—k
par. 3—i	par. 7—c	par. 11—d
par. 4—e	par. 8—a	par. 12—l

Using the Vocabulary: Suffixes (page 62)

Word endings can change the part of speech—a verb into a noun as students are asked to do in this exercise (*multiply - multiplication*), an adjective into an adverb (*active - actively*), a noun into a verb (*custom - customize*), or a verb into an adjective (*play - playful*). They can also change the meaning of a word (*careful - careless*).

A. Answers:

Verb	Noun
1. play	1. player
2. commission	2. commissioner
3. commit	3. commitment
4. retire	4. retirement
5. interrupt	5. interruption
6. manage	6. a. management b. manager
7. promote	7. a. promotion b. promoter
8. excite	8. excitement
9. exhibit	9. exhibition
10. own	10. owner

B. The word *spectacular* is an adjective. Today it is also used as a noun to mean something that is spectacular.

    spectacular (adj)—The band gave a *spectacular* performance.
    spectacular (n)—Tickets for the circus *spectacular* will go on sale on Friday.

C. Answers: 1. commissioner **2.** owns **3.** players **4.** manager **5.** retire **6.** excitement

Reading Tables (page 63)

The most important aspect of reading tables is paying attention to the headings at the top of each column. Often the information wraps from the bottom of one set of columns to the top of another.

◆ *Ask random questions about the table before starting this exercise. Sample questions might include "What is the range of years for this table?" (1980–1998) "What do AL and NL stand for?" (American League and National League) "Where was the All-Star Game played in 1995?" (Arlington, TX)*

Answers: 1. in 1985 **2.** (two) 2 **3.** (four) 4 **4.** CA (5) **5.** (twenty-one) 21

Expansion: Ask students to watch a sporting event on television and report back on the scores, the teams, and the highlights. Ask students to find out the scores from the most recent All-Star Game.

Thinking Together (page 64)

This type of activity is particularly important in a multi-skills class or in a conversation class where students need opportunities to interact with one another and practice speaking and listening skills.

The Race through History

Boston Athletic Association (page 65)

Preview notes: The picture on page 67 is of a famous organized event that attracts runners from around the world. The one on page 76 is of a much smaller local race. When they finish this reading, the students will be asked to write the topics on the line above each paragraph.

◆ *Have students read the directions on page 69, think about the topics as they read, jot down some phrases, and later go back and refine them. Remind them to formulate a topic that is not too broad or too narrow.*

Understanding the Reading: Identifying Topics (page 69)

Answers:

par. 1—the Boston Athletic Association

par. 2—the 100th anniversary exhibit of the Boston Marathon

par. 3—the influence of the Greeks on marathons

par. 4—the marathon distance

par. 5—Clarence DeMar, the winner of the most marathons

par. 6—amateur runners

par. 7—women in the marathon

par. 8—growth in popularity

par. 9—Bill Rodgers

par. 10—wheelchair racers

par. 11—retaining the traditions of the marathon

Using the Vocabulary: Word Forms (page 69)

A. Some adjectives that end in -ly that are not adverbs are: *friendly, lonely, only*

Verbs	Nouns	Adjectives
act	action	active
compete	competition/competitor	competitive
inaugurate	inauguration	inaugural
inspire	inspiration	inspirational
populate	population	popular
locate	location	local
profess	profession	professional
officiate	office	official
	spectacle/spectator	spectacular
	miracle	miraculous
	fame	famous

B. Answers: 1. famous **2.** inspire **3.** competitive **4.** miraculous/spectacular **5.** spectators

Thinking Together (page 70)

Answers: 11 players (soccer, American football); 9 players (baseball); 6 players (volleyball); 5 players (basketball); 2 players (tennis, beach volleyball, badminton, Ping Pong; these sports can also be played as doubles, with 4 players)

Keeping Track of Your Reading Rate (page 71)

Preview notes: Students may question the political correctness of the term "mentally retarded." Few people other than the Special Olympics still use the term "retarded" because it has a negative connotation. Alternatives that are considered more acceptable are "developmentally delayed," "mentally handicapped," "slow," or "mentally challenged." The word "disabled" has also been replaced by terms such as "physically challenged" or "physically handicapped." The term "people with disabilities" is also common.

Answers: 1. T **2.** F (It offers training in 22 official sports.) **3.** F (Experts had believed the mentally handicapped were not able to participate in sports.) **4.** T **5.** T **6.** F (Programs are year-round.) **7.** T **8.** F (Special Olympics helps people grow physically, mentally, socially, and spiritually.) **9.** F (Special Olympics is for adults and children.) **10.** T

Making Connections—Editing Your Work (Plural Nouns) (page 73)

♦ Tell students to check a learner's dictionary when they are unsure if a noun is count or non-count and remind them, too, that English writers generally use plural form when using a count noun in the general sense.

    I enjoy playing soccer. Soccer is a very healthy **sports**. The players have to run most of the **times**. Their **eyes** always concentrate on the ball. In this game, the players get tired very quickly. In a **competitions**, the players must wear **uniforms** to identify their teams. Usually they wear soccer **shoes** that have **sharps** edges. These edge**s** help the players run. They wear **shorts** and T-shirts with numbers on them. Each **players** has his name on his shirt to identify him to his coach.

CHAPTER 4
Staying Healthy and Fit

FOCUSING IN (pages 76 and 77, answers on page 272)

The photo on page 76 shows a group of older Americans warming up for a race. Five K and 10K races have become popular in the United States. These races are often fundraisers for worthy causes such as educational programs or cures for diseases, including MS (multiple sclerosis) and AIDS. Often there is an exercise program before the race, and participants can walk or run the distance.

The quote on page 76 is from a speech by Donna Shalala, who was the U.S. Secretary of Health and Human Services in the Clinton administration. The secretary is appointed by the president and approved by Congress. Divisions of the Department of Health and Human Services include the Food and Drug Administration, the Administration on Aging, the National Institutes of Health, and the Social Security Administration.

Body Ritual among the Nacirema
Horace Miner, *American Anthropologist*, June 1956 (page 78)

Preview notes: This article often appears in college anthropology texts and will probably be difficult for students to read. The photo on page 80 is of a "holy-mouth-woman," or a dental hygienist. The dental instruments on her tray are the "augers, awls, probes, and prods" referred to in paragraph 9.

◆ *Ask students to explain what an anthropologist is (a person who studies people, societies, and cultures) and to predict what they expect this reading will be about. Tell them that this is intended to be a humorous article, but that it might take them a while to "get the joke."*

◆ *Reinforce the advice in the prereading paragraphs by giving the students time to read the article quickly once to get the gist before they struggle with the details.*

Understanding the Reading: Reviewing Topics and Identifying Terms (page 81)

◆ *Make sure students have understood that this article is about body rituals of Americans before starting this exercise. If they have difficulty, explain some of the tricks the author has used to change the appearance of words.*

A. Answers: Overall topic: body rituals and health obsessions of the Nacirema

B. Answers: **1.** o **2.** i **3.** j **4.** l **5.** m **6.** b **7.** a **8.** h **9.** e **10.** n **11.** f **12.** g **13.** d **14.** c **15.** k

Using the Vocabulary: Dictionary Skills (page 82)

A. Alphabetizing: Alphabetizing is an important life skill, and this initial exercise will help prepare students to look up words in the dictionary.
paraphernalia, pathological, pathologist, pathology, phenomenal, practice, practitioner, prestige, protracted, purification

Expansion: If the class has not worked with dictionary skills before, use this page for an extra exercise as a preview. Learner's dictionaries, such as the *Longman Dictionary of Contemporary English,* provide ESL students with a wealth of information, such as which nouns are count (C=countable) and noncount (U=uncountable), which prepositions follow verbs, what phrasal verbs exist, in addition to sample sentences. Students have to be instructed in the use of these dictionaries for them to be useful.

Sample exercise:
- What part of speech is *pathetic*? (adjective)
- What do [C] and [U] stand for following noun definitions? (countable and uncountable nouns)
- Find one noncount noun. *(paraphernalia, pathology, pathos, prestige, purgatory)*
- What do [T] and [I] stand for following the *v* for *verb*? (transitive and intransitive verbs)
- On which syllable does the stress fall in the word *paramount*? (first syllable)

B. All of the answers come from the dictionary insert on page 83 from the *Longman Dictionary of Contemporary English*. Note that although the words are in alphabetical order, many words have been deleted in order to fit all the required words on the page.

Answers:
1. a. status deserving of respect **b.** prestigious **c.** U
2. a. relating to cause and effect of an illness; in this context, unreasonable and difficult to control due to mental illness. **b.** adjective **c.** pathology; pathologist **d.** pathogen, pathological, pathologist, pathos
3. a. noun **b.** practice
4. a. noncount noun **b.** Paraphernalia in the medicine cabinet might include toothpaste, medicine, makeup, pills
5. a. very unusual and impressive **b.** phenomenon **C.** phenomena

6. a. adjective **b.** Stress is on the second syllable. **c.** lengthy; extending for a long period of time **d.** removal of something dirty or unwanted **e.** purify

Thinking Together (page 85)

◆ *Have students review the list of phrases and words on page 82 before doing this exercise. Read some of the paragraphs aloud to see if the students can guess who or what is being described. Make a contest out of guessing the answer.*

Alternative Medicine Is Natural and Gives Patients More Freedom
Doris Williams, the *Salt Lake Tribune*, 9/20/94 (page 86)

Preview notes: Alternative medicine includes the use of herbal remedies rather than antibiotics and acupuncture and chiropractic medicine rather than pain killers and surgery. The facts in the margin notes on pages 90, 91, and 93 show the increasing interest in alternative medicine in the United States.

◆ *Make sure students understand the terms "alternative medicine" and "traditional medicine."*

Understanding the Reading: Annotating and Listing Information (page 88)

Students are asked to both mark their texts and write information on page 89. This exercise is the beginning of outlining, which will be dealt with more fully in Chapter 7.

Answers:
A. pars. 1 and 2: conventional Western medicine, alternative medicine
B. possible answers—par. 3: homeopathy, acupuncture, herbal medicine, energy medicine, naturopathic medicine
C. possible answers—par. 4: cancer, heart disease, rheumatoid arthritis, diabetes
D. They are from plants, minerals, and animals (par. 8).
E. par. 13, highlight the last sentence: According to the author, we need money "to investigate and test alternative therapies and educate our citizens accordingly."

Using the Vocabulary: Prefixes and the Roots of Words (page 89)

◆ *Point out to students that many scientific words are derived from Latin and Greek roots: psych- (mind), geo- (earth), therm- (heat) are some examples; ask them to come up with more.*
A. Answers: 1. b **2.** c **3.** a **4.** b **5.** c **6.** a **7.** a **8.** b **9.** c
B. Answers: 1. alternative **2.** procedures **3.** pharmaceutical **4.** prescribe **5.** arthritis

Reading Graphs (page 91)

Bar graphs are often used for a visual comparison among different groups.
Answers: 1. patients who did nothing for a health complaint, patients who went to the doctor, and patients who medicated themselves **2.** headache **3.** about 16 percent **4.** Most people ignored muscle aches. **5.** sore throat

Expansion: Have students work in groups to create more questions to ask one another based on the graph, or bring in another graph on health-related topics for more practice.

Reacting to the Reading (page 93)

Under the American system of health care, most people have insurance to help cover the cost of medical treatment. This insurance is usually paid for in part by their employers. Insurance companies, however, can deny benefits to a member if they do not feel that the treatment is justified or if it has not proven to be beneficial. Many insurance companies do not pay for acupuncture or chiropractic medicine. Most insurance companies will pay for prescription drugs, but not for herbal remedies.

Shape Up America!
Shape Up America! Organization, http://shapeup.org (page 93)

Preview notes: The surgeon general is nominated by the president and approved by Congress. His or her job is to act as chief general officer in the medical departments of the U.S. Army, Navy, or Air Force and to serve as chief medical officer in the U.S. Public Health Service. After resigning from his office, Dr. C. Everett Koop helped to found Shape Up America! because he felt that a nationwide program was needed to make Americans aware of the health risks associated with obesity and to offer information to help them get in shape. Their website at http://shapeup.org provides information on their mission and guidelines and plans to get in shape. Dr. Koop also has a website at http://www.drkoop.com.

Understanding the Reading: Annotating and Listing Information (page 96)

This exercise encourages students to develop a system of annotating (circling, underlining, or highlighting, as well as writing notes in the margins). They are also asked to transfer information to this page, which could later serve as a study guide for a test. Many students do not write in their textbooks because they have to return them (as in high school) or they plan to sell them after they use them.

♦ *Point out that highlighting too many things on a page becomes meaningless because they then have to read all of the highlighted sections.*

Answers:
A. Highlight the appropriate texts as indicated on pages 93 and 95.
B. In par. 2 (1) adult obesity rate—34 percent; (2) childhood obesity rate—21 percent.
C. In par. 2, hypertension, diabetes, heart disease, and cancer.
D. In par. 3—cost in lives—300,000 per year; cost in dollars—$100 billion per year.
E. Possible answers: exercising too little (sedentary push-button lives, driving everywhere), eating portions that are too big, eating fast food, maintaining an unhealthy diet, eating in a hurry.
F. In par. 10, walking, dancing, vacuuming, gardening.

Using the Vocabulary: Classifying Words (page 97)

This activity checks students' knowledge of the vocabulary words in the reading by asking them to identify words as indicators of good (physically fit = F) or poor (out of shape = 0) physical condition.

A. Answers: 1. 0 **2.** F **3.** 0 **4.** F **5.** 0 **6.** F **7.** F **8.** 0 **9.** F **10.** 0 **11.** F **12.** 0
B. Answers: 1. obesity **2.** diet **3.** exercise **4.** sedentary **5.** health

Thinking Together (page 97)

If you have access to computers, this quiz is located at http://shapeup.org. The answers are on page 276.

♦ *Encourage students to interview one another for this activity rather than to take the quiz individually.*

Keeping Track of Your Reading Rate (page 99)

Arnold Schwarzenegger is now a famous actor (star of the *Terminator* movie series), but he was once Mr. Universe, and he sponsors the Arnold Fitness Weekend described here. This reading explains his support of the health benefits of martial arts.

◆ *Go over the introductory information before starting the exercise, and review the tip which points out that focusing on important words, such as numbers and dates, is particularly important in reading academic materials.*

Answers: 1. T **2.** F (China) **3.** F (He is an actor.) **4.** F (1997 Arnold Fitness Weekend, of which the Martial Arts Festival is part) **5.** F (karate) **6.** T **7.** T **8.** F (about 15 million) **9.** T **10.** T

Making Connections—Editing Your Work (Parallelism) (page 101)

◆ *Remind students to pay particular attention to words joined by conjunctions such as and, but, or that should be in the same (parallel) forms.*

Self-improvement can be accomplished through ~~physically~~ **PHYSICAL**, mental and educational activities. According to the reading topic, Americans who never exercised in the past are now on the streets jogging, swimming, ~~dance~~ **DANCING** and practicing martial arts to improve their physical fitness and ~~reducing~~ **REDUCE** their stress. Others improve themselves by meditating quietly in their homes or ~~return~~ **RETURNING** to school to qualify for better jobs. In a nation where the rhythms of life are at a fast pace, people are seeking ways to find ~~peaceful~~ **PEACE**, tranquility, and most of all, a sense of accomplishment in their lives.

Additional Websites on Health

http://www.med.stanford.edu
http://nhic-nt.health.org
http://www.webmd.com

CHAPTER 5

Keeping the Beat

FOCUSING IN (pages 104 and 105, answers on page 273)

The picture on page 104 is of a rock concert on 5/22/94 in Montreal, Canada, by Pink Floyd, an English rock band known for such albums as *The Wall* and *Dark Side of the Moon*. The bright multilighted stage is typical of rock concerts, as is the electric guitar the lead singer is playing.

The quote is by Bill Cosby, one of the richest entertainers in the world. He started his career as a stand-up comedian, and his talent helped him win a role as the first African-American star in the TV drama "I Spy." That success was followed by his performance as Dr. Huxtable in the award-winning dramatic series "The Cosby Show." In 1970, he went back to college to study education and has since written several books. One of his favorite topics is the generation gap, which he shows is made wider by the younger generation's preferences for strange clothes and music.

Folk Music in America
Mercedes Hardey, http://users.aol.com/Jumpcity/folk.html (page 106)

Preview notes: Mercedes Hardey is a musician and ESL teacher in California. She is the founder and president of Cultural Horizons, and with the Notes on Harmony Family Music Program, she sings and plays guitar, as the picture on page 108 shows. She writes articles on the history of traditional music in America and, like many other folksingers, is dedicated to preserving cultural history through music.

Understanding the Reading: Listing and Mapping (page 110)

Organizing information into lists or designing schemas is a helpful study skill. It tests students' comprehension and helps them create a study guide. This exercise could be revisited after the exercise in outlining in Chapter 7 (page 165).

Possible answers:
Three themes: struggles and aspirations of common citizens, celebration of independence and freedom of expression, preservation of posterity, current events, changing morals and manners, love, the pioneer spirit, religion, and overcoming hardships
Kinds of folk songs: protest, love, traveling, blues, work, cradle, drinking, war, play
Titles of early American folksongs: "Yankee Doodle" and "On Top of Old Smoky" (par. 4), "Turkey in the Straw" (par. 9), and "John Henry" (par. 10)
Three characteristics (have students check the shaded box on page 107): unwritten songs, lyrics that reflect common speech, musical expression of ordinary people, usually from or by an unknown person or group, uncomplicated and unorchestrated music and lyrics, performed without musical accompaniment (or only acoustic instruments)
Five modern-day singers: Pete Seeger, Joan Baez, Theodore Bikel, Phil Ochs, The Kingston Trio, The Weavers, Malvina Reynolds, Buffy St. Marie, Bob Dylan (par. 14)

Using the Vocabulary: Vocabulary in Context (page 111)

This exercise extends the practice with the use of context clues that began on page 44 by pointing out the types of context clues often provided by writers.

A. Answers: 1. definition **2.** contrast **3.** experience **4.** comparison
B. Answers: 1. a **2.** b **3.** c **4.** a **5.** a **6.** b **7.** a **8.** a. **9.** c **10.** b
C. Answers: 1. fertile **2.** tenaciously **3.** modifications **4.** ballads **5.** jigs and reels

Thinking Together (page 113)

This exercise gives students a chance to work cooperatively to apply the criteria from the reading.
"We Shall Overcome" = protest
"My Bonnie Lies over the Ocean" = love
"Santy Anno" = traveling
"Things about Comin' My Way" = blues
"This Train" = traveling

Expansion: Bring in a tape of folk songs for the students to listen to. Consider introducing a variety of songs such as "Blowin' in the Wind," "Down in the Valley," "He's Got the Whole World in His Hands," "If I Had a Hammer," "Michael Row the Boat Ashore," "She'll Be Comin' 'Round the Mountain," and "This Land Is Your Land." Have students categorize the songs as they did in the previous exercise.

Expansion: In the United States, people begin learning folk songs at home, school, or church when they are quite young. Many folk songs are sung around the campfire. Ask students to sing a folk song they know or to make an oral presentation about where most people in their native countries learn or sing folk songs. Who are the people who teach them these songs? Are they teachers, parents, or leaders of church or youth groups? Where would a visitor to their countries be most likely to learn them or hear them? What kinds of instruments are associated with these songs?

True Blues and Country

Dan McGraw, *U.S. News and World Report*, 4/14/97 (page 115)

Preview notes: This article helps students understand two very American forms of music, blues and country, by taking them on a tour of two important cities in Tennessee: Memphis, once the home of Elvis Presley, and Nashville, home of the Grand Old Opry, where many aspiring musicians hope to be discovered. Two icons of American music that are mentioned in this article are Elvis Presley (1935–1977), the King of Rock and Roll, and B.B. King (1925–), the King of Blues. Every year fans flock to Graceland to honor Elvis's memory. His hits include "Love Me Tender," "Jailhouse Rock," and "You Ain't Nothin' but a Hounddog." B.B. King was first discovered in Memphis, Tennessee. He is famous for playing his guitar named *Lucille* and singing songs such as "The Thrill Is Gone," "You Shook Me," and "I Got My Mojo Workin'." In an interview in the *Charlotte Observer*, King states "Blues to me is many things. . . . It has to do with people, places, and things. And the way of life that we lived in the past, we are living today, and the way I believe we will live tomorrow. It tells you about the world as well; it tells you about yourself as well as the ones you love."

Understanding the Reading: Main Ideas (page 118)

Extending the skills worked on in Chapter 3 on topics, this exercise first asks the students to choose the correct main ideas and to explain whether the others are too broad or too narrow.

A. Answer: c
B. Answers: 1. par. 2—a (b is too broad) **2.** par. 5—a (b is too narrow) **3.** par. 6—b (a is too broad) **4.** par. 8—b (a is too narrow) **5.** par. 16—a (b is too narrow)

Using the Vocabulary: Participial Adjectives (page 119)

◆ *To help the students understand when to use past (V + ed/en/t) or present (V + ing) participles, tell them to ask themselves whether the noun being described is receiving or causing the action.*

A. Answers: 1. C **2.** I (sharecropping) **3.** I (daring) **4.** C **5.** I (checked)
B. Answers: 1. interesting **2.** bored **3.** entertaining **4.** remembered **5.** fascinated
C. Answers: 1. struggling **2.** interesting or fascinating **3.** bored **4.** fascinating or interesting **5.** guided or fascinating

Reading Maps (page 120)

Like the subway map in Chapter 1 (page 8), this exercise encourages students to work cooperatively to come up with solutions. Here they are asked to apply the information provided by the author to the map of Tennessee.

Answers: 1. T **2.** F (between Tennessee and Arkansas and Missouri) **3.** T **4.** F (near the Georgia border) **5.** F (no, because he took the long route on Highway 64)

Expansion: Tie this in to the **Responding to the Reading**, question 3, page 130 by having students use a map to point out cities where performers usually gather or give concerts in countries around the world (some possibilities include The Grand Ole Opry in Nashville or Washington Square Park in Greenwich Village in New York City).

MTV: Tomorrow the World?

Alan Bunce, the *Christian Science Monitor*, 2/16/89 (page 122)

Preview notes: Since this article was written, MTV has indeed expanded, as noted in the caption on page 123. It now offers an extensive array of music information. The website at MTV OnLine (www.mtv.com) has links to MTV news 1515 (a weekly news program), TV specialty shows, video newscasts, and listings for concerts, articles, and reviews. MTV also offers sponsors a yearly music festival. MTV has a global network of international affiliates: MTV Europe, MTV Latino, MTV Brasil, MTV Japan, MTV Asia, and MTV Mandarin.

Understanding the Reading: Main Ideas (page 125)

The ability to state the main idea is a critical, but difficult, skill. In the reading, "True Blues and Country," students were asked to choose the best of two stated main ideas for specific paragraphs. In this exercise, they are asked to choose the best out of three in part A and then to write their own main idea for the entire reading in part B. In the first reading in Chapter 6, "Never Too Old," they will continue to practice writing the main idea of paragraphs.

A. Answers: I. B II. C III. A IV. B V. A

B. Main idea: Since the universal language of music draws young people from all over the world together, MTV will become "hugely popular around the world."

Using the Vocabulary: Reviewing Compound Words and Participial Adjectives (page 126)

◆ *Go over the explanations of compound words and participial adjectives on pages 56 and 119 to remind students of the definitions and forms.*

A. Possible answers: cable television (par. 1); tv network (par. 1); pop culture (par. 3); broadcast (par. 4); viewpoint (par. 6); global network (par. 7); throughout (par. 8); comic book (par. 9); rock-and-roll (par. 14); Anglo-American (par. 15); cross-current (par. 16); cultural imperialism (par. 17); pent-up (par. 18); pan-European (par. 19); 24-hour (par. 19); music video (par. 24)

◆ *Remind students that compound words can be written as one word, as a hyphenated word, or as two words.*

B. Possible answers: *free-flowing* imagery (par. 2); *long-deferred* rewards (par. 5); *combined* power (par. 11); *unfounded* fear (par. 14); *American-produced* form (par. 15); *building* block (par. 26)

◆ *Warn students not to choose participles that are working as verbs in the passive voice or progressive or perfect tense forms.*

Expansion: For more practice identifying these words, use the first reading in this chapter ("Folk Music in America"), which has at least twenty participial adjectives and compound words.

Participial adjectives: (par. 2) *unrestrained* manner, *transplanted* European nationals, *contributing* factors, *fascinating* subject; (par. 3) *resulting* music; (par. 4) *pleasing* songs, *adopting* group; (par. 5) *drinking* songs; (par. 8) *emerging* sense; (par. 9) *British-based* song styles, *distinguished* history, *singing* newspapers; (par. 10) *railroading* songs; (par. 11) *sophisticated* . . . technology, *relaxed* pace; (par. 12) *self-seeking* materialism, *working* men; (par. 13) *consuming* desire, *worn* hands

Compound words: (par. 1) lifespan, folk music, folk songs; (par. 2) framework; (par. 3) foremost, homeland; (par. 6) hardworking; Anglo-Saxon; (par. 10) railroad(ing); (par. 11) time-efficient, sing-a-long; (par. 12) hard times; (par. 14) folksingers, modern-day

Thinking Together (page 127)

Keeping Track of Your Reading Rate (page 128)

◆ *Go over the introductory information before starting the exercise, and review the tip that points out that reading with a goal, in this case finding out what is special about d'Amboise's National Dance Institute, will help students focus their attention on the topic.*

Answers: 1. F (He grew up in New York.) **2.** T **3.** T **4.** F (It first started with boys only.) **5.** T **6.** F (He was a famous dancer first.) **7.** F (The goal is to help young children.) **8.** F (He has received at least the 5 listed here.) **9.** T **10.** F (There are institutes in cities around the country.)

Making Connections—Responding to the Reading (page 130)

Expansion: Have students present an oral report on a musician or group that they would like to know more about. Ask them to include video clips, pictures, tapes of songs, and any other interesting or relevant information.

Making Connections—Editing Your Work (Participial Adjectives) (page 130)

This exercise reviews participial adjectives by asking students to complete the phrases in context.

I love listening to the soundtracks of musicals such as *The Phantom of the Opera* and *Miss Saigon*. Almost always these songs are very **touchING** and filled with emotions. Just like a movie, a musical can present a story, but in a different way. With their complicated harmonies and beautifully **writtEN** lyrics, the songs carry the listeners into a **fascinatING** world of imagination. When I listen to Broadway music, I feel as if I am becoming a part of the story as I follow the **excitING** beats and flowing melodies. Thus, a musical song is like a combination of music, books, and movies, wonderfully put together that I can enjoy all at once by simply playing a CD. About a year ago, I also became a big fan of Rhythm and Blues. Whenever I hear the strongly **pronouncED** beat of an R and B song, I can't help singing along.

CHAPTER 6

Getting the Message

FOCUSING IN (pages 134 and 135, answers on page 273)

The photo on page 134 shows a special type of antenna that receives and transmits information from satellites. Some satellite dishes are now small enough to be placed outside a home window to receive television programs. The quotation from Lorne Bruce, a librarian, points out how telecommunications have opened up the information highway and allowed instantaneous transfer of information from one point to another. While the printing press, invented in 1450 in Germany by Gutenberg, provided a means for the mass production of books, the computer and the Internet provide a means for people to read via their computers a book that might be found only in a distant library. Note the other quotation by Bruce on page 145.

Never Too Old
John F. Dickerson, *Time* Magazine, Cyperspace Issue, Spring 1995 (page 136)

Preview notes: This article has been included to show the extent to which older Americans remain active. Senior citizen centers offer classes in computer literacy along with bingo and ballroom dancing. One person mentioned in paragraph 3, for example, is 75, but doesn't "want to be left behind by progress."

◆ *Discuss the availability of continuing education for senior citizens in other countries.*

Understanding the Reading: Reviewing Main Ideas and Annotation (page 138)

In Chapter 5 (pages 118 and 125), students were asked to chose the best statement of the main idea of paragraphs. In this exercise, they are asked to formulate a sentence that expresses the main idea of the paragraphs indicated. The topics have been provided to help them focus.

◆ *Remind students to ask the question: What does the writer have to say about this topic?*
◆ *Warn students not to make their statements too narrow or too broad, and emphasize that copying a sentence is not the same as capturing the main idea in a sentence of their own.*

A. Answers:
1. par. 2: (computers and senior citizens) Senior citizens are interested in and capable of learning how to use computers.
2. par. 3: (uses for the computer) Senior citizens use the computer for many purposes, from making greeting cards to starting businesses.
3. par. 5: (seniors, computers, and communication) Through on-line organizations such as SeniorNet, older Americans can communicate with a wide variety of people.
4. par. 7: (computers and connecting the generations) Computers provide a new means for younger people to gain information from older Americans. (Note: Point out that grandparents also learn from children, as can be seen in the picture on page 137.)
5. par. 8: (seniors and the digital age) Senior citizens are entering the digital age of computers in growing numbers.

B. Answers:
1. Circle Silver Fox Computer Club; underline 7,500 students
2. Circle AARP; underline 32 million members and 2 million computer users
3. Circle monitoring investments; tracking genealogy; producing memoirs; making greeting cards; performing legal research
4. Underline or highlight: "For many older people . . . ." and "They allow you to . . . ."
5. Underline the first sentence (main idea = Seniors are a growing group of computer users.)

Using the Vocabulary: Technical Computer Terms (page 138)

Note that many words that are part of our vocabulary today were not in use 20 years ago.

A. Answers: 1. cyberspace **2.** database **3.** e-mail **4.** Internet **5.** password **6.** websites **7.** modem **8.** network **9.** online **10.** usenet

O	N	F	U	A	P	C	N	O	S	T	R	X
N	L	F	U	Z	L	Y	F	Z	Y	D	Q	P
L	I	L	S	I	V	B	L	I	U	W	I	A
I	T	K	I	U	S	E	N	E	T	B	W	S
N	L	P	W	P	U	R	I	R	H	P	P	S
E	M	A	I	L	I	S	J	Y	M	T	G	W
P	E	S	N	K	C	P	O	N	J	M	B	O
C	D	A	T	A	B	A	S	E	M	L	P	R
O	P	Z	E	C	U	C	V	R	U	O	G	D
R	Q	B	R	R	G	E	Q	W	V	G	J	P
U	B	T	N	J	W	E	B	S	I	T	E	S
M	O	D	E	M	Z	J	F	R	K	N	O	A
H	N	E	T	W	O	R	K	K	A	B	R	W

B. Answers: 1. password **2.** Internet **3.** websites **4.** e-mail **5.** cyberspace

Thinking Together (page 140)

This exercise encourages students to examine the use of computers in their countries and in the United States.

Note: A Venn diagram is a set of two or more intersecting circles that allow students to fill in those details, facts, and examples that are specific to each domain by placing them in the separate circles. Those that are common to all the students will be placed in the intersecting area. In this exercise each circle represents a country.

◆ *Practice creating Venn diagrams with simple categories (fruit: orange/lemon) if students are unclear as to how to create one. There is also a sample on page 263 and another Venn diagram on page 224.*

Online Dating: Myth vs. Reality
Randy B. Hecht, *Match.Com News*, 8/6/97 (page 141)

Preview notes: The use of the computer to meet people may seem offensive to some students, especially those who fear the growth of cybersex-related websites. The question of censorship of the Internet is widely debated in the United States. Point out to students that even in the United States, activities seen as inappropriate uses of the Internet could jeopardize someone's job (as was the case for a Harvard professor of religion in 1999). Online dating, however, is seen as a harmless way to meet people, and its use is growing steadily (see the margin note on page 143). The address for the Match.Com website is www.match.com.

◆ *Survey the class before the reading to see how many students would consider meeting someone online. See if that number changes after the reading.*

Understanding the Reading: Fact versus Opinion (page 144)

Distinguishing between fact and opinion is an important reading skill. Although it is good for students to utilize their own background knowledge when reading, it is important that they learn to separate their previously held views from the points that the author is making.

B. Answers: 1. F (pars. 1, 4) **2.** O **3.** O **4.** F (par. 6) **5.** F (pars. 1, 2) **6.** F (par. 8) **7.** O **8.** O **9.** F (par. 8) **10.** O

Understanding the Vocabulary: Abbreviations and Acronyms (page 144)

◆ *Go over some well-known abbreviations and acronyms from the school or city you teach in before doing this activity.*

A. Answers: 1. INS = i **2.** CEO = j **3.** CPA = q **4.** CPR = h **5.** ETA = r **6.** KKK = d **7.** AIDS = f **8.** NAACP = m **9.** RSVP = g **10.** YMCA = s **11.** ASAP = c **12.** FBI = a

B. An example of each type of abbreviation is provided.

◆ *Allow students to look in a dictionary if necessary to find or check abbreviations.*

Expansion: Write a sentence with many abbreviated words in it and challenge the class to see who can decode it first (e.g., Drink 1 ltr. of H_2O and then go ASAP to meet the M.D. for your app. at 2 P.M. for an MRI). Ask the class to come up with others.

Reading Ads (page 146)

These ads follow the format of those found at the Match.Com website.

◆ *Make sure the students understand the key before tackling this exercise.*

Answers: 1. b **2.** c **3.** c **4.** b **5.** b

Thinking Together (page 148)

- *First go over the format of the ads on pages 146–147.*
- *Make sure students understand that they should create ads for fictional characters, not for classmates.*

Radio Activity

Peter Theroux, *Avenues*, January/February 1997 (page 149)

Preview notes: As the introductory paragraph suggests, radio and television talk shows have become increasingly popular in the United States. The most widely known is probably Oprah Winfrey's show (presented in the next reading on page 155), but others include *Larry King Live*, the *Tonight Show* with Jay Leno, *Late Night with David Letterman*, and *Rosie O'Donnell*. Radio programs range from the talk shows of political conservatives such as Rush Limbaugh to the more liberal ones on National Public Radio, such as *All Things Considered* and *Air Talk*.

Understanding the Reading: Fact versus Opinion (page 153)

This exercise reinforces the skill of distinguishing fact and opinion in the previous reading (there will be a similar activity on distinguishing between myth and reality on page 197).

- *Remind students to decide if something is a fact based solely on the information in the reading.*

A. Answers: 1. F (par. 1) **2.** O **3.** F (par. 4) **4.** F (pars. 16, 19, 23) **5.** O **6.** F (par. 13) **7.** F (par. 9) **8.** O **9.** F (par. 8) **10.** O

B. Answers:
KTNQ—1020 AM—all-talk Spanish Radio—Humberto Luna
KABC—790 AM—interview. celebrities—Michael Jackson
KMPC—710 AM—women's issues—Tracey Miller and Robin Abcarian
KLOS—95.5 FM—morning commute—Mark Thompson and Brian Phelps

Expansion: If English-speaking talk radio shows are available, bring in a newspaper listing of radio stations and programs. Test students' ability to scan by asking questions about the times, hosts, station names and frequencies, and programs; ask students to see if any of the hosts mentioned in the article are listed; have students listen to a show and report back on it.

Using the Vocabulary: Phrasal Verbs (page 154)

Like idioms, phrasal verbs require memorization. One verb, such as *get* in the example (or *take—take up, take on, take over*), takes on multiple meanings depending on the preposition or adverb that follows it.

- *Go over pages in a learner's dictionary and show students how to look up phrasal verbs.*

Answers: 1. listens to **2.** accounts for **3.** switch on **4.** tune in **5.** put in **6.** convert to **7.** shies away from **8.** talks back to **9.** call in **10.** heard about

B. Answers: 1. switch on **2.** tune in **3.** call in **4.** listen to **5.** talk back to **6.** shy away

Expansion: Walk around the class quizzing the students on phrasal verbs by presenting definitions and the verb and asking students to supply the preposition or adverb (example: *to rise out of bed / get ___*) or by just presenting the definition and asking students to state the phrasal verb.

Keeping Track of Your Reading Rate (page 155)

Oprah Winfrey started out as the host of the television talk show "A.M. Chicago" in 1984. By 1985 the program was renamed "The Oprah Winfrey Show," and it was broadcast nationally by 1986. Winfrey is a producer and also an actress and starred in *The Color Purple* (1985), *Native Son* (1986), and *Beloved* (1998).

◆ *Go over the introductory information and review the tip pointing out that reading in chunks will help students read more quickly and efficiently.*

Answers: 1. T **2.** F (She is bouncy and full of life.) **3.** F (The response was very positive.) **4.** T **5.** F (She says they get "a bad rap.") **6.** T **7.** T **8.** T **9.** F (It has been very successful.) **10.** T

Making Connections—Editing Your Work (Articles) (page 157)

In this paragraph, the singular count nouns *computer* and *career* require an article; the expressions *a lot of* and *one of the* + superlative require articles; and the noun *future* has an article since there is only one commonly known and agreed-upon future.

> Without the computer, we would still be in the Dark Ages. **THE** computer has helped people to have better lives and better living conditions. It can do things faster than people can. The computer has also helped advance our communication and transportation systems. As we become more advanced, we need more computer engineers to create a better world for **THE** future. There will be **A** lot of jobs for computer engineers. This is **AN** excellent career for someone who enjoys cyberspace. Computer Engineering is one of **THE** best majors for me.

CHAPTER 7

Making History

FOCUSING IN (pages 160 and 161, answers are on page 273)

This illustration of Uncle Sam is often used by the U.S. Army with the caption "I Want You!" As the introduction explains, it was supposedly Samuel Wilson (1766–1854) who was first called Uncle Sam. He was a meat packer from New England who supplied large shipments of meat to soldiers. Because the supplies were stamped "U.S." on the boxes, people began calling him "Uncle Sam." The idea that the shipments came from the federal government caused people to think that he symbolized the United States. The opening quote comes from Henry Miller, author of *Tropic of Capricorn* and *Tropic of Cancer*. These novels were initially banned in the United States and later became the focus of a series of obscenity trials; in 1964 the Supreme Court of the United States overruled state court findings on obscenity.

◆ *Ask students to discuss Miller's definition of a hero and to compare it to their own.*

Expansion: Ask students to discuss ways that heroes are remembered and honored around the world. In the United States, for example, highways (Martin Luther King Boulevard in NYC), airports (John Wayne Airport, California), schools (many John F. Kennedy High Schools), and bridges (the George Washington Bridge over the Hudson River) are named for heroic figures; many famous people are commemorated with postage stamps in their honor (for example, Eleanor Roosevelt and Elvis Presley).

The History of the American Red Cross
The American Red Cross Organization, www.redcross.org (page 162)

Preview notes: Americans actively participate in volunteer organizations of all types, from the workers for the American Red Cross to coaches for Little League Baseball and AYSO. U.S. presidents often inspire people to volunteer for programs such as the Peace Corps (John F. Kennedy), Habitat for Humanity (Jimmy Carter), A Thousand Points of Light (George Bush), and AmeriCorps (Bill Clinton).

Understanding the Reading: Outlining (page 165)

Outlining is an important academic skill, both for planning a piece of writing or organizing information from a reading. This exercise allows students to practice outlining by filling in the missing information.

  I. A. 1. **1863**
      B. 2. **Clara Barton**
 II. A. 2. **Water Safety**
        3. **First Aid**
      B. Mabel Boardman's philosophy: **"An ounce of prevention is worth a pound of cure."**
      C. 1. **Tending to the needs of the wounded and the sick**
      D. 2. **Tending to the needs of the able-bodied and disabled veterans**
          (other possible answers: Opening institutes for the blind and the crippled and contributions made in veterans' hospitals)
III. **The American Red Cross: Still the Greatest Mother in the World, 1920–1939**
      A. 1. Decrease in **volunteers**
      C. 1. **Floods**
        2. **Drought**
        3. **The Great Depression**
IV. A. 2. **Organizing blood drives**
      B. 2. **Gray Lady Service**
        3. **Junior Red Cross**
        4. **Hospital and Recreation Corp**
  V. **A New Frontier: Volunteers, Vietnam, and the Age of Technology, 1960–1979**
      A. 1. **Chemical plant accidents**
        3. **The first nuclear accident at Three-Mile Island**
      B. 1. **Veterans returning from Vietnam**
        3. **The elderly**
      C. 2. **A standard light blue uniform**
VI. A. Tradition: **Providing relief to victims of natural and man-made disasters**
      B. Public opinion: **1990s survey showing that the American Red Cross was the most highly regarded of major US charities and** *Money* **magazine naming the Red Cross one of the ten best-managed charities in the country**

Expansion: Ask students to outline another reading from this text, such as "The Race through History" (page 65) or "Keeping the Beat" (page 104 has information organized in a chart on page 110).

Using the Vocabulary: Suffixes (page 167)

This exercise continues the work on affixes and word forms that appeared in Chapter 3 (pages 62 and 69) and in Chapter 4 (page 89). More work on prefixes appears in this chapter on page 173.

A. Answers:

Adjective	Noun
able	ability
active	activity
charitable	charity
flexible	flexibility
neutral	neutrality
popular	popularity

Verb	Noun
assist	assistance
exist	existence
rely	reliance

B. Answers: 1. existence **2.** assistance **3.** activities **4.** neutrality **5.** flexibility

Thinking Together (page 168)

Other organizations include the Salvation Army (to alleviate human suffering); the American Medical Resources Foundation (to donate medical equipment to hospitals and clinics in developing nations); the International Eye Foundation (to help prevent blindness); International Service Agencies (to help people overseas and in the U.S. who suffer from hunger, poverty, and disease or from the ravages of war, oppression, and natural disasters); Girl Scouts and Boy Scouts (youth service organizations); Doctors Without Borders, USA, and Doctors of the World (medical volunteers).

Expansion: Ask students to find out what types of charitable organizations work in their areas, and to report on the type of help they are providing. Ask students to make a list of local problems that could benefit from volunteer services or from some other type of help.

Jackie Robinson
Avonie Brown, afroam.org (page 169)

Preview notes: Ballparks across the United States honored Jackie Robinson in 1996 in celebration of the 50th anniversary of his integration of baseball. The Baseball Hall of Fame in Cooperstown, NY, has a special exhibit for players from the Negro League and from the women's baseball league formed during WWII. Other athletes who have become American icons include Babe Ruth (baseball), Babe Didrikson (basketball, baseball, golf, track), Michael Jordan (basketball), Arthur Ashe (tennis), Peggy Fleming (ice-skating), and Tiger Woods (golf).

Understanding the Reading: Drawing Conclusions (page 172)

♦ *Remind students that they are to draw conclusions based only on what is provided in the reading, not on their own preconceptions.*

Answers: Check only numbers 2, 3, 4, 7, 8, 9, 13, 14, 15.
  1. No; he is a hero because he integrated the major leagues (par. 3).
  5. No evidence.
  6. No; Rickey's experiment had less to do with baseball and more to do with integration (par. 2).
  10. No evidence.
  11. No evidence; he attended UCLA, but we are not sure from the reading if he graduated (par. 3).
  12. No; Rickey only threatened to suspend players (par. 9).

Using the Vocabulary: Prefixes (page 172)

A. Answers: 1. a **2.** c **3.** a **4.** c **5.** a
B. Answers: 1. inevitable **2.** integrating **3.** Unlike **4.** interact **5.** illegal

Reading Timelines (page 174)

Answers: 1. Medgar Evers, Malcolm X, Martin Luther King, Jr. **2.** She refused to give up her bus seat. **3.** 1963 **4.** Lyndon Johnson **5.** 1962

Expansion: Divide the class into small groups to create timelines relevant to class topics. In this text, "The Race through History" (page 65) and "Cesar E. Chavez Biography" (page 225) lend themselves well to timelines. Use the timelines for a future quiz or assignment.

Thinking Together (page 175)

Note: Abraham Lincoln (1809–1865), the 16th president of the United States, wrote the Emancipation Proclamation, spoke out against slavery, and is credited with keeping the nation united during the Civil War. Susan B. Anthony (1820–1906) was a suffragist who fought for the rights of women to vote and to have equal employment, for children's rights, and for the abolition of slavery and the death penalty. Eleanor Roosevelt (1884–1962), "The First Lady of the Western World," wife of President Franklin D. Roosevelt, was a humanitarian and an author. She was appointed a delegate to the United Nations and traveled extensively as an outspoken messenger of peace and hope. Mohandas K. Gandhi (1869–1948), Indian peace activist, social philosopher, humanitarian, and writer, worked tirelessly to promote nonviolence throughout the world. Dr. Martin Luther King, Jr. (1929–1968), a minister, author, speaker, and civil rights leader, practiced the nonviolent teachings of Gandhi and worked to end the segregation of blacks in the United States. He received the Nobel Peace Prize in 1964. Mother Teresa (1940–1997), a Missionaries of Charity nun, received the Nobel Peace Prize in 1997 and spent her life helping the needy in the slums of Calcutta, India. She has been called a "living saint."

Expansion: Have students write short descriptions of well-known people whom they consider to be heroes, without using names. Ask them to read their descriptions aloud to see if other students can identify their hero.

Lawbreakers We Have Known and Loved
Robert McG. Thomas Jr., *The New York Times*, 5/16/93 (page 176)

Preview notes: The association between lawbreakers and "making history" is made because most of us think of heroes as law-abiding citizens, not outlaws. However, the daring actions of nonconformists also cause us to notice and often admire their bravery (or foolishness) and defiance of rules and regulations; risk-takers are remembered for their dangerous feats and adventurous, indomitable spirit. Even some criminals such as Bonnie and Clyde and Billy the Kid have become American legends.

Understanding the Reading: Drawing Conclusions (page 178)

It is important for students to understand that active readers draw conclusions as they read, and they adjust their conclusions as new information is revealed by the author. This exercises expands on the one on page 172.

◆ *Go over the instructions in italics before the reading, since this exercise requires students to stop and check off information as they read.*

Answers: The conclusions in paragraphs 1, 6, 7, 10, and 11 were confirmed.
par. 2—Never stated.
par. 3—Not confirmed, but implied.
par. 4—Not confirmed; Philippe Petit is French.
par. 5—No; defying gravity is daring but not always illicit.
par. 8—Not confirmed; Willig was fined only $1.10.
par. 9—Not confirmed; the punishment seems unlikely, but no one is sure.

Using the Vocabulary: Analogies (page 179)

Analogies are often used on standardized exams to test students' knowledge of vocabulary.

◆ *Go over the examples before asking students to do this exercise.*
A. Answers: 2. run **3.** river **4.** bad **5.** criminal **6.** government **7.** lawyer **8.** lovely/pretty **9.** murder/kill **10.** theft
B. Answers: 1. heroes **2.** risk **3.** teachers **4.** assassinated **5.** lionize

Expansion: Ask students to work with a partner to create some analogies of their own. Collect them and use them for a pop quiz.

Keeping Track of Your Reading Rate (page 181)

Amelia Earhart (1897–1937), American aviator, was the first woman to fly solo across the Atlantic Ocean (1932) and from Hawaii to California (1935). While she was attempting to fly around the world, her plane crashed in the Pacific Ocean (1937) and was never found.

◆ *Read the short introductory paragraphs before starting the reading, and review the tip that reminds students not to point their fingers or move their lips while reading.*

Answers: 1. T **2.** T **3.** F (She was a restless, individualistic feminist.) **4.** F (She promoted commercial aviation and the advancement of women.) **5.** T **6.** F (Her flights were well publicized.) **7.** F (She was a famous pilot before she married.) **8.** F (She had no plans to have children.) **9.** T **10.** T

Making Connections—Editing Your Work (Passive Voice) (page 183)

Passive voice is often used when describing a hero/victim relationship.

◆ *Go over the rules for the formation of the passive.*

> When my life was on the edge, my mom risked her life to save me. I can still recall the moment when we were on a boat sailing to America. Our boat ran out of fuel and the engine shut down. My mom gave me all her food that **WAS** left over. After a few days passed, we **WERE** rescued by a boat, but only a certain number of people could **BE** saved. With such a generous heart my mom told them to take me and she would stay behind. Luckily the decision **WAS** made to take everyone. Though some moms out there are the same as mine, I still think my mom is the best. Amelia Earhart and Rambo **ARE** not considered my idols. They do represent what heroes are, but my idol is someone that has done so much for me.

CHAPTER 8

Hitting the Books

FOCUSING IN (pages 186 and 187, answers on page 274)

The photo on page 186 shows a multi-cultural classroom of elementary school children. It is common to see American children sitting on the floor while listening to a story or sharing ideas and experiences. Students usually sit at tables of four to six children rather than at desks. The opening quote is by Henry B. Adams, who also wrote a nine-volume *History of the United States during the Administrations of Jefferson and Madison* (1889–1891).

◆ *Go over the chart on page 188 which provides a flow chart of the education system in the United States. Note that the dotted lines indicate educational paths not required by law. All U.S. students must be enrolled in school until they are sixteen years old; they are not required to complete high school, although in 1998 more than 80 percent of Americans over the age of twenty-five had a high school diploma.*

Turning the Corner: From a Nation at Risk to a Nation with a Future

Richard W. Riley, www.ed.gov (page 189)

Preview notes: The Secretary of Education is appointed by the president as part of his cabinet. Richard Riley served as secretary during President Clinton's administration. This is Secretary Riley's second annual State of American Education address (1995). While Riley admitted some of the shortcomings of American education, his purpose was to instill the hope in his audience that the United States was at a turning point, ready to tackle the task of improving the nation's future through better education. In paragraph 6, he outlined Clinton's Goals 2000, a specific plan for the new millennium.

Expansion: Ask the class to use the Internet to find a subsequent State of American Education address given by Riley. Find out how his focus changed between 1995 and the year 2000.

Understanding the Reading: Evaluating Evidence and Language (page 192)

This exercise calls for critical reading skills. Riley's speech is positive, but he does not always offer proof of the points he makes. It is important to note that in spite of all the promises, in paragraph 8 Riley reminds Americans that "the need to reduce the federal budget deficit must be balanced against our need to invest in America's future." In other words, the government will not go into more debt to improve education.

A. Answers:
1. check (par. 3; 7.1 million children)
2. check (par. 5; combined statistics)
3. check (par. 5; up 27 percentage points)
4. no check (par. 5; no data given)
5. no check (par. 5; no data given)
6. check (par. 6; 44 states)
7. no check (par. 7; polls mentioned, but no data given)
8. no check (par. 8; no evidence given)
9. check (par. 11; discoveries)
10. check (par. 13; details)

B. Inspirational phrases: turning the corner; a nation at risk to a nation with a hopeful future; the battle for excellence; getting the message; the stepping-stone to more learning; world-class graduates

Expansion: Try to get a recording or a videotape of a political speech, such as Kennedy's inaugural address or Martin Luther King, Jr.'s "I Have a Dream" speech. Play it for the class and ask students to write down phrases that are meant to stir the audience.

Using the Vocabulary: Word Forms (page 193)

This exercise reviews the suffixes and word forms learned in Chapter 3 (pages 62 and 69). The italicized words are all nouns.

◆ *Remind students to use the context to determine the correct word form needed and to use the correct verb forms.*

A. Answers: 1. *education:* (a) educate (b) educational (c) education **2.** *information:* (a) information (b) inform (c) informative **3.** *expectation:* (a) expectation (b) expect **4.** *cooperation:* (a) cooperated (b) cooperation (c) cooperatively **5.** *election:* (a) elect (b) election

B. Answers: 1. elections **2.** education **3.** expectations **4.** informative **5.** cooperation

Thinking Together (page 194)

This is a good exercise for those students who choose to do the second essay topic on page 210.

Standard Classrooms Aren't Necessary for Learning in Home School Program

Peggy Goetz, the *Irvine World News*, 6/5/97 (page 195)

Preview notes: This article is from a small city newspaper in California. It presents a positive report on local people involved in home schooling.

◆ *Take a poll of the class to see who thinks home schooling is a good idea and why. See if any views change after reading the article.*

Understanding the Reading: Myth versus Reality (page 197)

This exercise continues working on the critical reading skills of distinguishing fact versus opinion and drawing conclusions.

◆ *Remind students once again to concentrate on the message the author is relating, not on their personal views.*

Answers: 1. M (par. 8) **2.** M (par. 21) **3.** R (pars. 17, 28) **4.** R (par. 16) **5.** M (pars. 10, 11) **6.** R (par. 9) **7.** M (pars. 10, 26) **8.** R (par. 6)

Using the Vocabulary: Crossword Puzzle (page 198)

A. Answers:

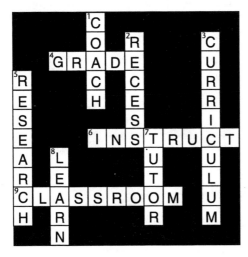

B. Answers:

◆ *Tell students that the words may not be used in the forms given (for this reason, only instruction, but not tutoring, is the answer for 2).*

1. creatively **2.** instruction **3.** tutors **4.** curriculum **5.** attend

Thinking Together (page 199)

Expansion: Allow students to have a debate between members of the class who advocate home schooling and those who oppose it.

Fresh Start—Adults Who Return to School and Life

Dennis Hevesi, *The New York Times*, **Education Life** supplement, 8/5/90 (page 200)

Preview notes: The caption for the picture on page 201 states that more than 40 percent of college students are twenty-five or older. This article helps show why so many adults return to college. Many universities offer continuing education and extension programs, such as the ones that Leo Gutkind and Karen James enrolled in. These programs allow students to attend college on a part-time basis without being formally accepted into a college until they have decided what degree to pursue.

Understanding the Reading: Charting Information (page 204)

Students did a less detailed chart activity on page 33. The chart that follows will be used later in this chapter (page 207) to create a written summary of the reading.

Name	Previous job	Special problem	College attended	Degree attained	Field of study	New job
Roy Eddington	thief	drugs	University of Massachusetts	B.A.	General Studies	counselor in Prisoners Against Drugs
Lee Gutkind	beer and soda truck driver; shoe salesman	poor grades; behavioral problems	University of Pittsburgh	B.A.	English (not directly stated)	writer; journalist; English professor
Barbara Patton	housewife	no skills; divorced; working single mother	Kingsborough Community College; Hofstra University	A.A. B.A. J.D.	Law	NY State assemblywoman
Karen James	hostess; saleswoman; messenger; proofreader	drugs; college dropout; divorced	Center for Early Childhood Ed; UCLA Extension	teaching certificate; paralegal certificate	Education; Law (plans to go to law school)	nursery school teacher; paralegal; supervisor

Using the Vocabulary: Figurative Language (page 205)

Understanding figurative language is particularly difficult for second-language students. There is a similar exercise in Chapter 10 on page 241.

◆ *Go over the explanation of similes and metaphors before asking students to do this exercise. Allow students to work with a partner.*

A. Answers: 1. "a spool that unravels new lines of possibility" **2.** cloth or fabric **3.** examples of successful students **4.** change her life **5.** made frequent trips back to jail **6.** going out to meet voters

B.

◆ *Do one of these as a class.*
Example: Continuing education is like a spool that unravels new lines of possibility.

C. Answers: 1. Roy Eddington **2.** Karen James **3.** Leo Gutkind **4.** Barbara Patton

Expansion: Bring in some poetry that contains many metaphors and similes. Read the poems aloud and ask the class to identify the figurative language used by the writer. Ask students to write their own poems incorporating images and experimenting with language.

Reading Schedules (page 206)

◆ *Remind students that reading a schedule is like reading a table (page 63) and that they must refer to the headings for the columns. In this case headings are on the first page only.*

Answers: 1. yes **2.** Basic Reading and Vocabulary **3.** yes **4.** ESL 6, ESL 10, Geology 1 and Geology 15 **5.** 3.5 credits **6.** room SM 47 **7.** one **8.** 1.5 hours a week **9.** both **10.** code 2236

Expansion: Distribute copies of your school's schedule of classes. Ask the class to create questions about it. Ask students to use the schedule to explain their own program and the courses they are taking, or have them quiz one another about their schedules (e.g., "If I take Bio I on Wednesday, who is the instructor?").

Keeping Track of Your Reading Rate (page 208)

◆ *Go over the introductory paragraph on Albert Shanker first, and then remind students not to pause too often while they read this passage.*

Answers: 1. T **2.** F (He was the only Russian Jew among Irish and Italians.) **3.** T **4.** T **5.** F (He attended public schools.) **6.** T **7.** F (He never completed his dissertation.) **8.** F (They were poor immigrants.) **9.** T **10.** F (He was honored for his work.)

Making Connections—Editing Your Work (Word Forms) (page 210)

Students have done a number of exercises on word forms. This exercise tests their ability to find errors in context.

> When taking a test, many people form what's called "test anxiety." Test anxiety is **FEAR** of ruining the test. Test anxiety is a problem for students who have to take many tests. As a student myself I take many exams, and every time I take the tests I get test anxiety. I think "what if I do **POORLY** on the test?" Once I had to take the SAT test. It was a big test. Of course I had to do well because it would put me into a college. The pressure on me was **ENORMOUS**. Once I started the test, I wasn't **ABLE** to remember anything. It was in my head, but I was so **NERVOUS** the things I had studied were flooding my head, so obviously I did badly on the SAT test.

CHAPTER 9
Climbing the Corporate Ladder

FOCUSING IN (pages 212 and 213, answers on page 275)

This picture shows a business meeting in which corporate employees gain global information via satellite. Note that while this is a formal business meeting, according to a 1998 *New York Times* poll compiled by David Wallis, a majority of Americans now dress informally for work. Today, workers are required to keep up with technological advancements such as computers, pagers, fax machines, and scanners. The quote is by W.H Auden, a poet and playwright, who was born in England but lived most of his life in America. His words reflect the American work ethic and the fact that the identity of even the richest American is tied to the work he or she does (also see the proverbs on page 237).

The New Way We Work
Martha Groves, the *Los Angeles Times*, 2/26/96 (page 214)

Preview notes: American workers go back to school to learn new trades and update their skills at adult-education and community colleges, job training programs, technical institutes, and corporate universities. In the June/July 1999 issue of *Your Money* magazine, senior editor Christine Verdi states that over 2 million students each year are educated in about 6,000 career schools. According to Richard Koonce, author of *Career Power!,* the best job insurance is continuous training.

Understanding the Reading: Charting Information and Paraphrasing (page 216)

This exercise reviews the use of charts as organizational tools (see exercise on page 204). Paraphrasing tests student understanding of reading material and helps them avoid plagiarism.

◆ *Go over the directions to this exercise carefully and do the first two items as examples. Remind students that their decisions must be based on the information in the article.*

A. Answers:

Workers' expectations to . . .	20 years ago	Today
need continued job training	↓	↑
work for one company all their lives	↑	↓
make a mid-life career change	↓	↑
return to school after college	↓	↑
advance easily in a company through hard work	↑	↓
work from 9 to 5	↑	↓
need to know about technology	↓	↑
do their own typing	↓	↑
work in a culturally diverse environment	↓	↑
have more than one skill	↓	↑

B. In this exercise students have to choose between two options, but on page 222 they will be required to write their own paraphrases.

Answers: 1. a **2.** a **3.** b **4.** b **5.** a

Using the Vocabulary: Hyphenated Modifiers (page 217)

Hyphenated modifiers are related to compound words and illustrate the changing nature of language.

A. Answers: 1. f **2.** g **3.** j **4.** c **5.** i **6.** h **7.** e **8.** d **9.** b **10.** a

Expansion: Have students work in pairs or small groups to list other hyphenated modifiers. Ask them to scan "Radio Activity" (page 149) and "Fresh Start—Adults Who Return to School and Life" (page 200) and highlight more hyphenated modifiers.

Reading Graphs (page 218)

This is the second of three graphs that focus on understanding visual information (see pages 92 and 251).

Answers: 1. Agriculture, fishing **2.** Operators/factory workers/laborers, Precision production, and Administrative support **3.** Administrative support **4.** Agriculture/fishing and Technicians **5.** Professional specialty

Expansion: Assign students to bring in examples of pie graphs that pertain to one of the topics that have been covered in this book plus three to five questions they have developed about the graphs. Use them in a quiz.

Thinking Together (page 219)

When discussing the definitions of the terms "white-collar" and "blue-collar," remind students that white-collar jobs are usually those that require recognized college degrees, credentials, or certificates. White-collar workers may include dentists and dental hygienists, pharmacists, doctors, nurses, lawyers, teachers, engineers (aerospace, computer, electrical, chemical, and mechanical), secretaries, salespeople, travel agents, and accountants. Blue-collar workers include assembly-line workers, auto mechanics, plumbers, construction workers, dock workers, painters, carpenters, bricklayers, and coal miners.

Happy Workers a Must
Jan Norman, the *Orange County Register*, 8/29/92 (page 220)

Preview notes: The author writes about employers who motivate their workers by granting them recognition and respect. This may include giving employees incentives such as pay raises, stock options, and a percentage of gross profits. It may also mean improving day-to-day working conditions and creating a positive environment. According to the people interviewed, making employees feel worthwhile increases productivity. Additional perks offered by some companies are training and rapid advancement, signing bonuses, and longer vacations.

Understanding the Reading: Paraphrasing and Making Inferences (page 222)
Like drawing conclusions (page 178), making inferences is a critical reading skill.
A.
◆ *Ask for volunteers to write their sentences on the board for class discussion, since many of their answers will be different depending on the techniques used.*
B. Answers: 1. T **2.** F (Pars. 6, 7, and 8 inform us of the profits and productivity gained when employers put their workers' concerns first.) **3.** F (Pars. 6, 7, 8, and 22 stress the importance of caring for workers' concerns.) **4.** T **5.** F (Pars. 2, 3, 5, 12, 13, and 23 give examples of different types of positive feedback.)

Using the Vocabulary: Classifying Words (page 223)
Sorting words thematically helps students gain a better understanding of vocabulary.
A. Answers: 1. N **2.** P **3.** P **4.** N **5.** N **6.** P **7.** N **8.** P **9.** P **10.** P **11.** N **12.** N **13.** P **14.** N **15.** P **16.** P **17.** N **18.** P **19.** P **20.** N
B. Answers: 1. gloomy/bad moods **2.** unproductive **3.** complaints **4.** motivation/enthusiasm **5.** in the doldrums **6.** lift morale/keep morale up **7.** incentive **8.** token of gratitude **9.** profits **10.** rewards/raises

Cesar E. Chavez Biography
The California Curriculum Project, *Hispanic Biographies* (page 225)

Preview notes: Migrant workers are day laborers who move according to the seasonal need for agricultural help. In addition to Chavez, champions for the rights of American workers include Albert Shanker (see page 208), Samuel Gompers (first president of the AFL), and George Meany (first president of the CIO). As part of their campaign for civil rights around the world, Mahatma Gandhi and Martin Luther King, Jr. helped secure better conditions for workers. Workers' rights is the theme of many songs by folksingers mentioned in Chapter 5, including Woody Guthrie, Joan Baez, Bob Dylan, and Phil Ochs.

Understanding the Reading: Sequencing (page 228)
Putting events into chronological order tests students' ability to understand the material.

Year:	Order:	
1880	1	Cesario Chavez crossed from Mexico to the United States.
1937	3	The Chavez family lost its farm.
1927	2	Cesar Chavez was born.
1938	4	The Chavez family moved to California.
1944	5	Cesar Chavez joined the U.S. Navy.
1948	7	Cesar became a teacher to migrant workers.
1962	8	Cesar Chavez began to work organizing farm workers into a union.

Year:	Order:	
1973	10	The National Farm Workers Union became the United Farm Workers of America.
1948	6	Cesar Chavez married Helen Fabela.
1965	9	Grape pickers went on strike.
1978	11	The boycott on grapes and lettuce was lifted.

Expansion: Type up a list of events that are part of story or a historical piece. Cut the list into separate sections and have students put them in chronological order. Ask students to list the events in another reading, "Return to Ellis Island" (page 4) or "Lawbreakers We Have Known and Loved" (page 176), in chronological order.

Using the Vocabulary: Finding the Meaning from Context (page 228)

◆ *Remind students of the ways they have learned to figure out the meanings of words from the context (pages 44 and 111).*

A. Answers: 1. c **2.** a **3.** b **4.** a **5.** c **6.** a **7.** b **8.** a **9.** c **10.** b **11.** c **12.** a
B. Answers: 1. boycott **2.** strike **3.** confrontation **4.** neglect **5.** recruit

Thinking Together (page 231)

Some of the possible answers students may list are the AFL–CIO (American Federation of Labor–Congress of Industrial Organizations), which has many more affiliated unions such as the United Auto Workers, the American Postal Workers Union, the American Federation of Government Employees, and the American Federation of Teachers (AFT). Students may also list international unions such as the ETUC (European Trade Union Confederation), the ICFTU (International Confederation of Free Trade Unions), the APRO - ICFTU (Asia Pacific Regional Organization), and the ORIT - ICFTU [Latin America Regional Organization (in Spanish)]. A more complete listing can be found at http://www.aflcio.org/unionand/unions.htm.

Expansion: Ask students to review the reasons Caesar Chavez organized a union for the crop workers. Then discuss the mission statement of the AFL–CIO on page 230 and ask them to summarize ways unions benefit workers other than farm laborers.

Keeping Track of Your Reading Rate (page 231)

◆ *Make sure students understand what a home business is, and then go over the tip about keeping the main point of the article in mind while reading.*

Answers: 1. F (She has commuted to work for several years.) **2.** F (She was living in New York City.) **3.** T **4.** F (She's an Artists' Representative.) **5.** F (Her commission is 15 percent.) **6.** F (She and her husband plan to have children.) **7.** T **8.** T **9.** F (She talks about separating work and home life, feeling the pull of unfinished tasks, and keeping phone calls brief during her work days.) **10.** T

Expansion: Encourage students to have a debate on the pros and cons of working at home.

Making Connections—Editing Your Work (Verb Forms) (page 233)

I've **DONE** many volunteer jobs that are **RELATED** to the medical field. Last summer I volunteered at a doctor's office and had the chance to talk with the doctor about my career choice. The doctor, who is a friend of my parents, is a successful man. He works at a popular hospital in our community. He told me that becoming a doctor was not about money but about **HELPING** people. He said, "If you want **TO MAKE** a lot of money, you should **BECOME** an engineer." He advised me to decide on the profession that matched my goals in life. It was good advice.

CHAPTER 10

Pursuing Happiness

FOCUSING IN (pages 236 and 237, answers on page 275)

This is a photo of a family preparing to go away on a summer vacation. According to the Travel Industry Association of America, the average summer vacation by car lasts a little over a week and covers over 600 miles. The quote by Bastienne Schmidt, a German photographer who works in New York, comes from a special *New York Times Magazine* issue (6/8/97) entitled *How the World Sees Us*. The photo captures one of the traditional pleasures that the American family still enjoys.

The Pursuit of Happiness: Once Upon a Time, Did More Americans Live Happily Ever After?

Leslie Dreyfous, the *Salt Lake Tribune*, 9/13/92 (page 238)

Preview notes: The shelves of American bookstores are filled with self-help books, as illustrated in the photo on page 239 (see sample titles on page 258, number 7). Esalen was founded in 1962 as "an educational center devoted to the exploration of unrealized human capacities" (www.esalen.org). Other types of retreats focus on religion, marriage and family, or health.

◆ *Ask students first to look over the **Thinking Together** instructions on page 244 so that they can underline or highlight appropriate references as they read.*

Understanding the Reading: Review (page 241)

This exercise and the one on page 248 follow the format of a standardized reading test.

Answers: 1. b **2.** b **3.** c **4.** b **5.** c **6.** a **7.** b **8.** b **9.** c **10.** b

Using the Vocabulary: Figurative Language (page 243)

The use of imagery and idiomatic expressions creates mental pictures that add descriptive details.
A. Answers: 1. b **2.** a **3.** a **4.** a **5.** b **6.** b **7.** b **8.** a **9.** a **10.** b

Expansion: Ask students to share similar expressions and sayings from their own languages. Then have them work in pairs or small groups to write short descriptions using some of the sayings.

Thinking Together (page 244)

Some of the themes include references to topics such as these: in paragraph 5, science and technology (Chapter 6); in paragraph 5, equality and civil rights (Chapters 3 and 7); in paragraph 6, health and beauty (Chapter 4); in paragraph 8, work (Chapter 9); in paragraphs 9, 17, and 18, marriage and family (Chapter 2); in paragraph 16, communication (Chapter 6); and paragraphs 11 and 26, finding happiness (Chapter 10).

Pursue Your Passion

Shari Caudron, *Industry Week*, 9/2/96 (page 245)

Preview notes: According to a 1997 *U.S. News*/Bozell Worldwide poll, 49 percent of Americans said society put too much emphasis on work and not enough on leisure; 8.5 percent of Americans worked 60 hours or more per week. Margin notes in this chapter include many statistics on ways Americans spend their leisure time. Other hobbies include shopping (more than 185 million people visit the 20,000 malls around the United States each month, according to the International

Council of Shopping Centers), golf (according to a National Golf Foundation survey in 1998, participation in golf was 26.5 million), and travel both inside and outside of the United States (the most popular foreign countries to visit in 1998 were Mexico, Canada, and the United Kingdom).

Understanding the Reading: Review (page 248)

Answers: 1. a **2.** c **3.** b **4.** b **5.** c **6.** c **7.** a **8.** c **9.** b **10.** b

Using the Vocabulary: Reviewing Analogies (page 249)

This exercise reinforces the one on page 179.

A. Answers: 1. c **2.** c **3.** a **4.** b **5.** b

B. Answers: 1. fulfillment **2.** burned out **3.** hobby **4.** enthusiastic **5.** rekindle

Expansion: Bring in samples of TOEFL, SAT, and MAT tests for additional practice with analogies.

Reading Graphs (page 250)

This exercise expands on the practice with graphs (bar graph on page 92 and pie graph on page 218).

Answers: 1. golfing **2.** picnicking and driving, running or fishing **3.** walking **4.** golfing **5.** 19 percent

ONU Habitat for Humanity

Margaret Dwiggins, the *Courier*, 3/12/96 (page 252)

Preview notes: During spring break in March 1998, Palm Springs offered a renaissance festival, an arts festival, and several jazz festivals. Daytona Beach has a website for spring break activities at http://www.daytonabreak.com. Even so, as this author points out, many students spend their mid-semester vacation doing volunteer work; others take part in special academic programs or travel.

Understanding the Reading: Paraphrasing and Summarizing (page 254)

A.

INFORMATION ON HABITAT FOR HUMANITY

Abbreviation	HFHI
Founders	Millard and Linda Fuller
Year founded	1976
Number of houses built/renovated by 1996	40,000
First college campus with a chapter	Baylor University (Waco, Texas)
Interest rate for loans on the house/materials	Zero percent
Former U.S. president involved in the organization	Jimmy Carter

B.

♦ *Ask for volunteers to write their sentences on the board for class discussion since many of their answers will be different depending on the techniques used.*

C.

◆ *Choose one group to compose their short summary on the board and critique it with the class.*

Using the Vocabulary: Crossword Puzzle Review (page 255)

Expansion: Have students work together in groups to create their own crossword puzzles. Make copies of some of the best ones and distribute them as exercises or incorporate them into quizzes.

Keeping Track of Your Reading Rate (page 256)

◆ *Read the first paragraph and the reading tip that reminds students to look over the comprehension questions at the end of the passage before reading the passage in order to find the answers more quickly.*

Answers: **1.** T **2.** F (She says it's heaven.) **3.** F (They take vacations in August.) **4.** T **5.** F (Summer is still the busiest time.) **6.** T **7.** F (They take extended weekends or shorter vacations.) **8.** T **9.** T **10.** T

Making Connections—Editing Your Work (Verb Tense Shifts) (page 258)

I have many friends who have different pastimes, but most of their hobbies are in sports, video games, computers, and so on. Photography is my all time favorite hobby. When I am depressed, desperate, or bored with my daily routine, I pick up my photographic equipment and **BEGIN** my adventure.

My grandfather, who **WAS** a photographer back in the early 1900s, also **HAD** a huge photography studio, but I never saw it because it was torn down during the invasion of China. When I was small, I **LOVED** to play with cameras. Perhaps my skill was inherited from my grandfather because now whenever I see something interesting and beautiful then I naturally imagine a picture in my brain. I get my equipment together and I **TRY** to get a better perspective of it.